40 Days of Encouragement

40 Days of Encouragement

Terry D. Slachter

To order additional copies of this book, contact:
Xlibris Corporation
1-888-795-4274
www.Xlibris.com
Orders@Xlibris.com
72791

CONTENTS

This book is dedicated to all the many people in my life who have encouraged me along the way.

INTRODUCTION

In the Bible, the number forty seems to be a recurring number for a period of time God used to exercise the faith of His people. In some cases, as in the wilderness wanderings, the time frame was forty years. For others, it was forty days and even forty nights (i.e. Noah, Elijah, the city of Nineveh, and even Jesus).

A forty day (or year) period seems to be an adequate period of time for faith to be exercised and tested, usually in the context of spending time in the wilderness away from the hustle and noise of city life. Life out in the wilderness wasn't easy or convenient for the people living in Biblical times. And, if given a choice, they would have preferred busy city life. But for those who endured the refining fires while in the wilderness testing periods; they returned with the reflection of the Refiner's face.

There are times in our lives today when we feel as though we are being led out into a wilderness of sorts. Our wilderness experiences may include periods of physical sickness, discouragement, depression, persecution, loneliness, and anxiety-filled waiting. Times like these call for us to be still and listen to the Lord, finding strength in Him.

If you are going through such a time, this forty day study booklet will help you find strength from His word and encouragement through the testimonies of other Christians. Even a church fellowship struggling through issues will find this booklet a useful tool for finding encouragement while in the wilderness periods. I want to suggest three practical ways to utilize this booklet for both personal and group settings.

1. **For a personal daily devotional**. Read the daily scripture passages and devotional that follows. The additional scripture passages and questions that follow each devotional are designed to help the reader consider the theme for each

day through the lens of other scripture passages. Readers who make time to read and consider each of these additional passages will find their time well spent.

2. **For small group use**. Have group members read through the daily devotions on their own, but then use the additional scripture passages and questions as the basis for group discussion. The questions are inductive in nature, and will force group members to examine each passage in the light of the daily scripture passages and themes.

3. **For a church-wide encouragement emphasis**. Use the materials as a five week "encouragement emphasis" time within the church. Plan sermons, Sunday school classes, and small group meetings using the themes and additional study questions offered in this booklet. The forty devotions are organized around five topics: the nature of Biblical encouragement; the nature and attributes of God; Biblical Promises; Biblical word pictures of encouragement; and the inheritance of God's children. These five topics could be used as sermon themes for five consecutive Sundays as an introduction to the weekly theme.

DAY 1

What is Biblical encouragement?

Reading: I Samuel 23:7-18

David had become a fugitive in the land of Israel. Had Saul lived in our day, "Wanted" posters of David would be placed in every post office and, perhaps, even a prime time spot on the television show, "Saul's Most Wanted". Saul's jealousy and his fits of rage made David a wanted man in his own land; a land he would soon reign over as the next king.

I don't think many of us know what it is like to be on the run and in hiding for over twelve years. We can't even begin to imagine what it would be like, always looking over our shoulders with fear, viewing all people with suspicion (I Samuel 23:12).

But David didn't need to worry when he met with his friend, Jonathan, in the context of today's passage. Jonathan came as an encouragement-medic to the tired, and stressed out, future king of Israel. He also came at a great risk towards his own safety. Jonathan's father, Saul, had already killed eighty-five priests and had laid waste to an entire town for conspiring with David, public enemy #1. But Jonathan goes to the wilderness anyway, where David is hiding, in order to help him find strength in the Lord.

My friends, this is the key for understanding the Biblical concept of encouragement. When we are weak and discouraged, we too need to be infused with God's strength to march on in the Christian life. At the heart of encouragement is God: to know Him more intimately, to know and be reminded of His word and promises daily, and to know the love of His people as they rally around us in His name.

This will be our pleasant journey in the next 40 days. Who knows what stressful situations, what serendipitous surprises, or what Saul-like stalkers will pass your way in the days ahead. Be encouraged in the fact that God already knows what lies ahead and that He will give you the strength needed to deal with it all. He may even send you an encouragement-medic, like Jonathan whom he sent for David, who will help you find strength in the Lord.

The scripture passages on the next page are intended as a source of encouragement for you today as you consider how the Lord brings encouragement to His children. These passages also remind us of our role as encouragement-medics; to comfort with the same kind of comfort we have received from the Lord.

For further study and discussion

Psalm 10:12-18 (vs. 17)
How does God encourage the afflicted according to this passage?

John 11: 17-26 (vs. 19)
How do the Jews comfort Martha and Mary? How does Jesus comfort them?

Romans 1:8-13 (vs. 12)
What does Paul mean by mutual encouragement?

I Thess. 2:1-16 (vs. 12)
What are the differences between encouraging, comforting, or urging in this context?

I Thess. 4:13-18 (vs. 18)
What particular words or thoughts do you find encouraging in this passage?

DAY 2

Healing

Reading: Acts 27:27-44 (vs. 36)

As a pastor, I frequently visit with patients in hospitals. And, quite often, the patients are attached to drip lines used for infusions of fluids and medicines, and sometimes blood, bringing healing and strength to their ill bodies. These infusions are essential when patients are bleeding and/or unable to orally ingest medicine. Without these medical lifelines, the patients have little hope of renewing their physical strength and getting well.

Or, perhaps you have witnessed paramedics or doctors rushing to the scene of an accident. They might start an I.V. in the arm of a person whose strength and life are quickly hemorrhaging away. The earthly bodies God has blessed us with require the life-sustaining flow of blood pumping into our heart, lungs, and brain in order to function properly. Fluids and other medicines are regularly needed to keep our bodies alive and healthy, also.

What is true in the physical world is also true in the spiritual world. In the context of our reading today, we see Paul acting as a spiritual E.M.T. on this ship feared to be heading toward the rocks. Since many had gone the fourteen days without eating, Paul knew that tensions and stress levels were high aboard this ship. Some sailors were even ready to secretly sail away on the lifeboats and avoid the possibility of crashing the boat ashore.

But, before the sailors could fool the soldiers and escape, Paul alerted the soldiers on board to cut the ropes of the lifeboats in order to be saved. Then, before all of the crew, Paul shared what an angel had shared with him several days earlier (vs. 23). He encouraged them by a word of hope (*"not a hair from the head of any of you shall perish"*) vs.34 and by exhorting them to eat. Paul's words and the bread he offered were an infusion of strength as their courage and hope were hemorrhaging away. Verse 36 tells us that they were all encouraged by Paul's words and example.

One of the Greek words for encouragement is euthymos. You might recognize the word when you sound it out because our English word, enthusiasm, comes from it. Euthymos literally means putting strength into someone. In the context of the reading today, this was Paul's purpose. And this is what we are called to do for others. A biblical word of hope and a faith-filled example may be needed today by some tired co-worker or family member. Are you prepared to give an encouragement transfusion today if someone near you collapses with fear? Read through some of the "healing" passages listed below and consider how you can bring healing to others this week.

For further study and discussion

Proverbs 12:13-19 (vs. 18)
What enables another person's words to bring healing?

Proverbs 15:1-14 (vs. 4)
If deceitful words crush the spirit, what kinds of words bring life?

Isaiah 58:1-9a (vs. 8)
What is the connection in this passage between light and healing?

Malachi 4: 1-3 (vs. 2)
What does righteousness have to do with healing?

Matthew 4:23-25 (vs. 23)
What do Jesus' healings tell us about his nature?

Revelation 22:1-6 (vs. 2)
What connection or purpose do the leaves have with the healing of the nations?

DAY 3

Refresh

Reading: Philemon 1:1-7

"*Refreshments will be served after the ceremony!*" When was the last time you heard the word "refreshments" used in this way? It seems too formal for everyday use. In fact, if you called your family to gather around the dinner table, they would think it odd if you did so by yelling out "*Evening refreshments are now being served in the dining room!*"

In today's reading, Philemon 1:1-7, The Apostle Paul uses the Greek word ana-pauo, which means rest, relaxation and refreshment. In the ancient Greek world, ana-pauo would have described the rest and relaxation soldiers needed when coming off the battlefield. Jesus also uses a form of this word when he describes the type of rest the gospel message offers to hearts that are burdened with heavy yokes. His yoke is easy and light, and the soul yoked beside him will find true refreshment (Matthew 11:28-30). The Apostle John uses this word to describe the "rest of the saints", who are with the Lord in heaven, resting from their labors (Revelation 14:13).

Paul writes Philemon this letter, asking this well-to-do Christian man and friend of his for a favor. He asks that Onesimus, a runaway slave of Philemon's, be accepted back into Philemon's household and into the church of Colosse. He asks this favor because Onesimus is now a Christian, converted by Paul. But before Paul asks this favor, he commends Philemon for his great love to others.

It was a love that reached the ears of Paul, bringing him joy and encouragement.

Paul was told about how Philemon "refreshed" the hearts of the saints. Here was a man who enabled fellow Christians to rest from the rigors of missionary service, or the trials of suffering, by simply opening his home and his heart to them. Consequently, these people were blessed deep down in their hearts as they witnessed this influential man's unconditional love for them without even making them feel embarrassed or obligated to repay him. It was truly a little taste of heaven as they spent time in Philemon's home and in fellowship with him.

Living the Christian life can be overwhelming at times. We fight spiritual battles, we diligently serve and love others, and we endure painful trials that burden our hearts while exhausting our strength. We need a little taste of heaven's refreshments. These kinds of refreshments often begin when someone sacrificially ministers to our needs with a glow of Christ-like love.

For further study and discussion

I Kings 19:1-9 (vs. 7)
Why is food an important part of Elijah's recovery?

Psalm 89:19-29 (vs. 21)
How did God sustain David through the years?

Jeremiah 31:23-26 (vs. 25)
How does God refresh weary people? How has he refreshed your strength in the past?

Matthew 4:1-11 (vs. 11)
How do you suppose the angels refreshed the battle-weary Jesus?

Mark 5:35-43 (vs. 42-43)
Why did Jesus think it necessary to tell the girl's parents to feed her?

Acts 3:11-26 (vs. 19)
What are times of refreshing according to this passage?

DAY 4

The God of Comfort

Reading: II Cor. 1:3-7 (vs. 3)

It doesn't take much to comfort children. An old, worn out blanket, or a germ-infested pacifier quickly ease any suffering or discomfort a child might experience. Clara Null wrote in "The Christian Reader Magazine" about one particularly stressful day she had when raising her small children. "It was one of the worst days of my life; the washing machine broke down, the telephone kept ringing, my head ached, and the mail carrier brought a bill that I had no money to pay. Almost to the breaking point, I lifted my one year old into his high-chair; I leaned my head against the high chair tray and began to cry. Without a word, my son took his pacifier out of his mouth and stuck it in mine." The child was simply sharing his "comfort" with his mother.

Paul shares with the Corinthians how he had suffered for the sake of the gospel (II Cor. 4:7-12, 6:3-10, 7:2-7, 11:16-33, 12:7-10). But he doesn't share his sufferings with them in order to solicit sympathy or to receive applause because of his bravery. No! Paul shares his sufferings in order to encourage them in the sufferings they were facing and would continue to face in the future. Paul found great comfort in the God of all comfort, and it's with this same comfort he could comfort them.

Paul will use the Greek word for comfort or encouragement, parakeleo, some ten times in this chapter alone, with seven more uses found in the rest of this letter. We shouldn't be surprised because we also see the Greek words for suffering and trials used seven different times in this same first chapter of Second Corinthians. Paul talks a lot about suffering, but rarely outside of the context of God's comfort.

God is the God of all comfort (II Cor. 1:3). And, by experience, Paul knew this aspect of God's character. God is the very essence of comfort because His nature is love and compassion. Man was created to enjoy God and to share in His great love. Through fellowship with Him and clinging to Him in our trials, we experience the joy of His presence. It is this joy of the Lord that renews our strength (Nehemiah 8:10). And, because God is the God of *all* comfort, no matter what trial we face in our lives, He will comfort us with the right kind of comfort at *all* the right times, and with *all* of His power.

For further study and discussion

Psalm 119: 49-56 (vs. 50)
What promises of God have encouraged you in the past?

Isaiah 40:1-5 (vs. 1)
How are the people comforted in this passage?

Isaiah 51:1-6 (vs. 3)
How does this passage bring comfort to God's people?

Jeremiah 31:10-14 (vs. 13)
How does God's comfort bring joy?

I Corinthians 14:1-5 (vs. 3)
How do prophecies bring encouragement and comfort?

Philippians 2:1-9 (vs. 1)
How does union with Christ instill courage and comfort into the life of a Christian?

DAY 5

Be Still!

Reading: Psalm 37:1-15 (vs. 7)

We need vitamins and minerals to supplement our daily diets because we don't eat the right kinds of foods that contain all of the essential vitamins and minerals our bodies need. The same is true for encouragement. We seldom get enough encouragement in our day to keep us strong and positive about life. Let's call it Vitamin E. We need to take daily supplements for this, and these can only come from God. God is handing them out, but are we truly listening?

Before refrigerators were invented, icehouses were used to preserve perishable foods. These icehouses had thick walls, no windows, and tight-fitting doors. Large blocks of ice were obtained during the winter and placed in the icehouse. During the summer months, the blocks were covered with sawdust.

One day a man lost his very valuable pocket watch while working in the icehouse. He and his fellow workers diligently searched for the valuable time piece to no avail. A small boy heard of the problem and quietly slipped into the icehouse. He soon emerged with the valuable watch in his hand. The men were amazed at how quickly this boy had found the watch. In fact, they felt a little foolish that a single boy found it after a group of men searched for it! They asked him how he found it. "Shucks," he said, "it wasn't too hard to figure out. I closed the door, laid down in the sawdust, and kept very still. Soon I heard the watch ticking; . . . tick, tick, tick, tick.

And I was able to go right to where it had fallen in between two blocks of ice."

Do you need some encouragement today? If you can, stop what you're doing, remaining still and listen. Listen closely and carefully. You'll find it best to not go through the motions of listening to God like some visiting dignitaries had done at the White House with former President Roosevelt. F.D.R. was sick of the small talk and, in fact, believed that no one really listened to what he was saying half the time. So, one day, he put his theory to the test. As people stepped forward to greet him, he told a number of them, "I murdered my Grandmother this morning." And, sure enough, many walked by saying things like: "That's nice", "How lovely", and "Keep up the good work". Finally, one foreign diplomat actually listened and told F.D.R., after F.D.R. told him about the murder of his grandmother, "Mr. President, I'm sure she had it coming to her."

Again, don't go through the motions with God when trying to hear His voice. Listen for the still, small voice of God that may come through the words of other Christians. This voice is sent by God to bring you comfort. Listen, also, for God's voice through the Spirit's work in our hearts. And, by all means, listen for God's voice through His own words from the Bible.

For further study and discussion

Exodus 14:5-14 (vs. 14)
What does it mean to be still in this passage?

Deuteronomy 27:1-10 (vs. 9)
Why did Moses and the Priests instruct the people to be silent before the Lord?

Psalm 46 (vs. 10)
Why do we have to be still in order to know God?

Habakkuk 2:18-20 (vs. 20)
Why is it important for man to be still before a holy God? What is the alternative?

Zechariah 2 (vs. 13)
Why is man called to be still before God here in this passage?

Mark 4:35-41 (vs. 39)
Why were the disciples terrified when Jesus calmed the stormy sea and made it still?

DAY 6

He Carries Us!

Reading: Psalm 68:1-20 (vs. 19)

The first half of Psalm 68 contains many references to the times God rescued Israel and brought her out of Egypt into Canaan, culminating with the ark being placed in Jerusalem. God's throne is placed in the temple, at the very center of David's city. God is the real king over Israel.

But the second half of Psalm 68 goes on to give praise to the King of Kings who subdues all of His enemies and even makes them fall to His feet in worship. He deserves praise from all the kingdoms of the world. Therefore, Israel can rejoice and be assured that the awesome God will give power and strength to His people. That includes His chosen people of today; the Church.

We should find great encouragement in these words, but sometimes these words don't sink easily into our minds or into our hearts. That is why the scriptures are full of word pictures that help us to meditate on the person, and the promises of God. In Psalm 68:19, we see a powerful word picture that illustrates the theme of this entire Psalm. God is the one who daily bears, or lifts, our burdens. Our mighty God, who "rides the ancient skies above", and who "thunders with a mighty voice", actually stoops down to lift us up.

There are times in our lives when we think the whole world rests on our shoulders. Our burdens can become very heavy as we try to carry the entire load ourselves, that we feel like fainting. Henry Moorhouse, a Scottish preacher, was going through some very difficult trials in his life. His young daughter, Minnie, became paralyzed and bound to a wheelchair. Henry was devastated and felt overwhelmed by all of the circumstances in his life. But, one day, as he came home with a package for his wife, his daughter met him at the door. "Where is Mother?" Henry asked. "Upstairs," Minnie replied. "Well, I have a package for her," Henry said. "Let me carry it to Mother," the little girl said. "Why, Minnie, how can you carry this package? You cannot carry yourself," Henry said. With a big smile, the child replied, "Oh, no, Papa; but if you give it to me, then I will carry the package, and then you can carry me." The Lord used her words to gently remind Henry that no matter how heavy the burden he was carrying, the Lord was daily carrying him.

Enjoy reading the other passages of scripture below. Let them remind you of God's care and love. He is the God of all comfort who understands and carries us every step of the way.

For further study and discussion

Numbers 11:4-17 (vs. 12, 17)
Have you ever felt like Moses, carrying the weight of the world on your shoulders? What are the negative effects of this kind of weight lifting?

Deuteronomy 1:26-33 (vs. 31)
What is the context of this passage?

Deuteronomy 33:7-12 (vs. 12)
How is God's comfort and care pictured in this passage?

I Samuel 2:1-10 (vs. 8)
Who does God lift up in this passage? Has God ever lifted you up from an "ash heap"?

Isaiah 40:6-11 (vs. 11)
What does it mean to be near the heart of God?

Isaiah 53 (vs. 4, 6)
What kind of sorrows does the Lord carry in the context of this passage?

DAY 7

Casting Your Cares on Him

Reading: Hebrews 4:14-16 (vs. 16)

Do you ever feel as though no one understands what you are going through? You might feel like no one can empathize with you or your current situation. You are unique, and no matter what people say or do, they don't seem to understand. No one knows what to say or how to bring help or comfort. Don't be too sure about that!

When Mitch Albom, a well-known sports writer from Detroit, heard that his favorite college professor was dying, he sought to renew their friendship. Albom admits that he hadn't seen Morrie Schwartz, his old professor and friend, for some twenty years. But, that didn't matter. Morrie was dying because of complications from Lou Gehrig's disease. Mitch felt drawn to Morrie's side.

In fact, Mitch visited Morrie weekly, and his meetings became the basis for a popular bestseller entitled, "Tuesday's with Morrie". And, with each visit, Morrie shared insights and humor that Mitch felt were worthy of sharing with the rest of the world.

During one of their conversations, Mitch asked Morrie why he bothered following the news since he wouldn't be around to see how things would turn out anyway. In response to that question, Morrie offered the following insight about empathy:

> **"It's hard to explain, Mitch. Now that I'm suffering I feel closer to people who suffer than I ever did before. The other night on TV I saw people in Bosnia running across**

29

**the street getting fired on, killed, innocent victims. I just
started to cry. I feel their anguish as if it were my own. I
don't know any of these people. But, how can I put this?
I'm almost drawn to them."** *

Now, let me ask you again. Are you sure no one in this world
understands what you are going through? As Mitch Albom noticed
with his friend, Morrie Schwartz, people who suffer are able to
empathize and be drawn to the hurt and pain of others.

One more question for today. If a human being like Morrie
Schwartz can be drawn to the plight of suffering people in Bosnia,
people he doesn't even know, than how much more will Christ
Jesus, who knows you personally, be drawn to you and your troubles?
Listen to these words from Hebrews chapter 4:14, found in the
Bible: **"For we do not have a high priest who cannot sympathize
with our weaknesses, but one who has been tempted in all things
as we are, yet without sin."** The passage ends with encouragement
for you and for me. Since Jesus has gone through what we are
experiencing, we can pray to him with confidence knowing that
he will give us exactly the grace and strength we need in our times
of hurt and pain.

If you are struggling today with a trial or an ongoing illness, and
you are tired and weak, take some time today (or even right now)
to share it with Jesus. Tell Jesus what's going on in your life and ask
him for his mercy. He knows exactly what you are going through.

For further study and discussion

Psalm 55:12-23 (vs. 22)
How does the Lord sustain the righteous?

Psalm 94:12-25 (vs. 19)
How is God's consolation different than the world's version of consolation?

Ecclesiastes 11:7-10 (vs. 10)
Why should we cast off anxiety according to this passage?

Nahum 1:7-15 (vs. 7)
How have you experienced God's care in the past? Why is it hard to put our trust in His care?

Luke 12:22-31 (vs. 31)
What things will be given to us if we first seek his kingdom?

I Peter 5:5-10 (vs. 7)
What does it mean to cast our cares upon him? Do you ever take back your cares?

Day 8

The Most High God

Reading: Daniel 4:1-18 (vs. 17)

I don't know about you, but I'm bothered by people who arrogantly wave their fist in the air, defying both God and man. You know the type! The kind of arrogance that made the Soviet cosmonauts in their early space flights boldly claim, "We went into space and we didn't bump into God!"

There have been others with this arrogance throughout the years. For example, people like Voltaire, the French philosopher, who made arrogant claims against Christianity. Even though he thought there was some cosmic power greater than man, he didn't believe in Christ. In fact, he predicted that Christianity would be swept away and would pass into history within one hundred years of his lifetime!

Voltaire died in 1778. Some fifty years later however, the Geneva Bible Society bought, and moved into, Voltaire's house, using his own printing press to produce thousands of Bibles that were distributed worldwide; so much for his arrogant claims, boasting about Christianity's imminent extinction! Who can say God doesn't have a sense of humor?

There was one other man who waved his fist into the air with arrogance. His name was Nebuchadnezzar, the proud king over the Babylonian empire. Even after he was warned by God's prophet Daniel to humble himself, he refused. God cut him down to size by making him insane for seven years. In that time, this mighty king

Nebuchadnezzar lived like an animal out in the fields. When God finally restored him, his final message to the world was this:

"For His dominion is an everlasting dominion, and His kingdom endures from generation to generation. And all the inhabitants of the earth are accounted as nothing, but He does according to His will in the host of heaven."
(Dan. 4:34-35)

If you wonder why God doesn't do something about the bullies of this world, don't fret. The things they do and the pride they exhibit will not go unnoticed or unpunished by God. God always gets the last word. And, in the case of Voltaire, he also got his printing press. Enjoy reading and meditating upon the passages below. Revel in the fact that God is the Most High God. He's the one who really calls the shots!

For further study and discussion

Genesis 14:18-24 (vs. 20)
What does the "Most High" God do for Abram?

Psalm 7:6-17 (vs. 10)
How does God shield us today? What is/was the purpose of a shield for battle?

Daniel 3:13-30 (vs. 26)
What does it mean to be a servant of the Most High God? Are you a servant of the Most High God?

Daniel 4:28-37 (vs. 34)
How did Nebuchadnezzar honor the Most High God? Why is this so significant?

Daniel 5:18-31 (vs. 18, 21)
How does Daniel describe the Most High God here in this passage?

Acts 16:16-19 (vs. 17)
Why is it significant that the demonic living within this slave girl uses the title "The Most High God"?

DAY 9

A Compassionate God

Reading: Exodus 22:21-27 (vs. 27)

In the midst of all the laws from everything concerning property, slaves and sex, we find three laws that reflect God's heart of compassion. The stranger in a foreign land, who didn't know a single person, was lost, lonely and limited in resources. The widow and orphan in that same culture were hard-pressed to find their daily sustenance and were often abused. And the hard-pressed soul, who gave his outer cloak for collateral toward a loan, would freeze at night if it wasn't returned to him by the money lender.

These weak and helpless people were protected under the national laws God established with His people. But, if these laws were not fulfilled, and the alien, widow, orphan, or the freezing-cold borrower cried out to God, God's promise to them was, "I will certainly hear them!" God's ears are especially tuned to the cry of society's poor and destitute because of His compassion.

But, when we think of God's compassion, we must do so in its broadest sense because God is also compassionate and slow to anger with us concerning our sins (Psalm 103:8, 13). As a father, He hears the cries of troubled souls mourning over their sins and failures. God had the same kind of compassion for Ruth and Naomi, who were left poor and destitute, as He had for Ruth's great grandson King David, who sinned miserably in God's eyes (Psalm 32). In fact, God has compassion for you today no matter if you are rich or poor. Remember that God hears your cries today!

We must also see God's compassion as an active and limitless source of help. In our day, compassionate people who advocate for the poor and abused, or who try to alleviate suffering, do so within limits. The Salvation Army bell ringers stand before busy stores trying to fill red kettles. Relief agencies are forced to show starving children on television to touch our hearts and open our wallets. But God's kettle is never empty! And His power to touch a hurting heart with a blessing or to provide relief in the nick of time is guaranteed. Because God is compassionate, I can be assured that His heart aches with mine today. Take some time to read about God's compassion in the passages listed below.

For further study and discussion

Nehemiah 9:5-28 (vs. 19, 27-28)
What makes God's compassion so great in the context of this passage?

Psalm 103: 1-19 (vs. 8, 13)
How does the Psalmist describe God's compassion in this passage?

Isaiah 54:1-10 (vs. 7, 8, 10)
Why does God continue to demonstrate His compassion to sinful people?

Matthew 14:13-21 (vs. 14)
How does Jesus show compassion to the crowd? How have you enjoyed his compassion in your life?

Luke 15:11-24 (vs. 20)
How does the father in this parable demonstrate his compassion for his lost son? What does this parable teach us about God's compassion?

II Corinthians 1:3-7 (vs. 3)
What is the connection between compassion and comfort?

DAY 10

Our Heavenly Father

Reading: Matthew 7:7-12 (vs. 11)

Douglas Heiman, from Evansville Indiana, worked on a home that was owned by a Rev. Jones, a retired United Methodist Church pastor. Rev. Jones told the story of God's provision for him and his wife in the midst of hurricane Katrina. Rev. Jones' daughter had begged her father to leave New Orleans, and drive north to Atlanta in order to ride out hurricane Katrina. The hurricane was brewing in the Gulf and headed straight toward Louisiana. The only problem was that Rev. Jones had no money readily available. To be sure, he had money in the bank, but it wasn't open. Rev. Jones was without cash and had no way to get to his daughter's home.

When the hurricane hit, Rev. Jones and his wife left their home and went to a shelter. After the storm had passed, they were allowed back into the city to retrieve a few belongings from their flooded home. When they entered the house, water was still to their knees, but Rev. Jones was determined to retrieve what he could salvage.

As he made his way through the house, he saw several framed family pictures floating in the water. He really didn't see anything else worth saving, so he grabbed the pictures and left. Back at the shelter, he took the photos out of their frames. Behind one of the pictures he was surprised to find money. It was a picture of his father, who had died when Rev. Jones was only 12 years old. He had no idea that the money was behind the picture and he doesn't know who put the money there. Did his father place the money in the picture back in 1942?

As Rev. Jones counted the money, he was surprised by the amount: $366. In fact, it happened to be the exact amount of money needed for Rev. Jones and his wife to buy two tickets to fly up to their daughter's home in Atlanta. Whether it was Rev. Jones' father who had placed the money in the frame, or someone else, we know that ultimately our Father in heaven placed that money there for the Jones' to have.

God is good and He knows what we need to get through each day, and even what we need to survive in the aftermath of a storm. And isn't it assuring to know that God never short changes us. He gives us exactly what we need. I hope this story of Rev. Jones has encouraged you to put your trust in the Lord. He will never fail you.

For further study and discussion

Isaiah 64 (vs. 8)
On what basis does Isaiah ask the Lord to not be angry forever with their sins?

Matthew 5:43-48 (vs. 48)
What is the nature of our Heavenly Father? How is it demonstrated in this world?

Matthew 6:25-34 (vs. 26, 32)
What does this tell us about God's fatherly love and care?

Galatians 1:1-5 (vs. 3)
How does our Heavenly Father give grace and peace to us?

Ephesians 1:1-8 (vs. 3)
What are some of the spiritual blessings our Father gives to us through Christ?

Philippians 1:1-11 (vs. 2)
Has the Father begun a good work in your life? How does the promise in verse 6 bring encouragement and hope to our hearts?

DAY 11

Our Jehovah

Reading: Philippians 4:10-20 (vs. 19)

One of Church histories greatest prayer warriors was a man by the name of George Muller. Muller lived in the 1800's in England, spending most of his life in the city of Bristol. Muller was a pastor who refused to collect a salary, believing that members would not cheerfully give for a pastor's salary. He trusted the Lord would provide for all of his needs; this would be Muller's life story.

In 1836, Muller and his wife started an orphanage in their own home with thirty girls. The work continued for several years, and by 1870, he was caring for more than two thousand children. But, through it all, he never made any requests for financial support nor did he ever go into debt.

George Muller never asked for money except through prayer. But there were many times when his faith was tested. For example, on one occasion, funds were running low to buy food for the many orphans under his care. He kept praying persistently, and sleeping very little. On the first day of his prayer marathon, nothing happened. On the second day of his prayer vigil, there was still no money. On the third day, there were still no signs of any money about to appear. Finally, on the fourth day, a woman stopped by the orphanage with a huge contribution after hearing about Muller's work. The amazing thing is that this woman had gotten lost and was wandering around the city for four days.

Thinking about this incident, Muller wrote the following observation: **That the money was so near the orphanage for**

41

several days without being given, is a plain proof that it was from the beginning in the heart of God to help us; but because the Lord delights in the prayers of his children, he allowed us to pray so long and also to try our faith and make the answer so much sweeter.

Muller also had a passion for missionary work. He founded the "Scripture Knowledge Institution for Home and Abroad" with the goal of raising money to buy bibles for schools and missionaries. Again, money was never solicited, nor were funds from the government sought. Through prayer, this organization received and disbursed over 1.5 million pounds, or about 2.7 million dollars in U.S. currency, for the work of missions and schools. That was an amazing amount of money for that time period, especially when you consider they prayed for every last cent.

Sometimes we wonder in awe at the faith and persistence of a man like George Muller. But he served the same God who is willing to make us abound with his resources in order to do his work. He is Jehovah-Jireh (the Lord who provides). Be encouraged today as you meditate on the person and work of our Lord. The Lord is also our Jehovah-Rohi (the Lord our Shepherd), our Jehovah-Shalom (the Lord our Peace), and He is Jehovah-Nissi (the Lord our Banner).

For further study and discussion

Genesis 22:1-8 (vs. 8)
How will God ultimately provide the lamb for Abraham, and for us? And, at what cost?

Judges 6:11-24 (vs. 24)
How does the Lord give peace to Gideon's heart? How does He give peace to our hearts today?

I Corinthians 10:1-13 (vs. 13)
According to this passage, what else does the Lord provide for His children?

II Corinthians 2:12-17 (vs. 14)
What else does the Lord give to us according to this passage?

II Corinthians 9:6-14 (vs. 8)
What does Paul mean when he tells us that God will make all grace abound to us?

I Peter 5:1-4 (vs. 4)
What will be given out when the Chief Shepherd returns? And to whom?

DAY 12

Our Unchanging God

Reading: Hebrews 13:1-8 (vs. 8)

If you have read through the Bible, you are aware of the many accounts of how God rescued people from lion's dens, fiery furnaces, and tumultuous storms. But have you ever wondered whether or not God rescues people today from danger, or from the storms of life?

Before the United States entered the World War II, the Japanese were expanding their empire into China. Their attacks upon the Chinese were cruel and relentless. But before the Japanese occupied China, another force occupied parts of China. Christian missionaries came not with guns or military might, but through deeds of love with the message of Jesus.

One of these "occupiers" was a single lady by the name of Gladys Aylward. She had been a missionary to China for more than 50 years before the Japanese came. And, with a heart of love, she taught Bible stories from village to village. However, the war would change her ministry and challenge her faith. Hundreds of children were left orphans because of the war. Gladys adopted many of these children as her own. And when she was forced to leave her home of Yangcheng, she had over a hundred orphans to care for and protect!

As Gladys and the children crossed the mountains and the Yellow River for the safety of Siam, the journey proved to be frightful. At one point, Gladys fell into deep despair and panic. She came to the conclusion that they would never reach Siam. But then a

13-year-old girl from the group of orphans reminded Gladys of a much beloved story. The story of how God helped Moses and the children of Israel cross over to safety through the Red Sea. In a fit of rage, Gladys snapped back at the 13-year-old, "But I'm not Moses!" The young girl responded by saying, **"Of course you aren't, but God is still God!"***

That word of encouragement helped Gladys because she kept marching forward with her young band of orphans, making it all the way through the mountains into Siam. They proved once again, that no matter how powerless or helpless we feel, God is still God and we can trust him to help us, even in today's perilous times.

For further study and discussion

Genesis 21:22-34 (vs. 33)
Who did Abraham call upon in this passage? Why is the term "eternal" used with God's name?

Psalm 90 (vs. 2)
How does the knowledge of God's eternal nature bring comfort to the Psalmist's heart here in this chapter?

Psalm 100 (vs. 5)
How can this passage bring assurance to the hearts of today's parents?

Psalm 102 (vs. 25-27)
How can this passage be used to encourage someone going through the grieving process?

Lamentations 3:19-26 (vs. 22)
What is the context of this passage? How can Jeremiah be confident of God's continued love and faithfulness?

Daniel 7:9-14 (vs. 9, 13)
Who is with the Ancient of Days here in this passage? How does this passage bring us encouragement to face the challenges of our time?

DAY 13

"Yes"!

Reading: II Corinthians 1:18-22 (vs. 18, 19)

Many people know the name Paul Bunyan, the fictional logger who did everything in a big way. But have you ever heard of John Bunyan? John Bunyan wrote the familiar story entitled, "The Pilgrim's Progress".

John Bunyan lived in the 1600's under the pressure and persecution of the English government, who refused to give religious freedom to believers outside of the state run, Anglican Church. Bunyan was arrested numerous times for preaching without the authority or consent of the Anglican Church. He was imprisoned for a period of twelve years for this crime.

But it was in the confines of the county jail in Bedford that he wrote his great Christian allegory, "The Pilgrim's Progress". The story is about a man named Christian who is progressing to the celestial city (heaven). As he continues to move ahead, he meets certain people and obstacles, and even encounters locations, that represent the issues of the Christian's life.

On one particular occasion, Christian and his friend, Hopeful, are captured by a giant, named Despair. The two of them are thrown into the dungeon of Doubting Castle and are beaten severely. The giant's wife, named Gloom, told her husband to induce such hopelessness in the lives of the two prisoners that they begin to think about suicide. He told the prisoners their fate: "No more food, daily beatings, and that their only hope was suicide."

Finally, as Christian and Hopeful were praying, Christian remembered that he had a key with him to unlock the prison doors, called Promise. "What a fool I am, to lie here in this stinking dungeon when I might walk free on the highway to glory!" And sure enough, the key called Promise opened the doors and they both escaped.

John Bunyan knew what dark and hopeless prison cells were like. Because he had the keys of Promise, he rose above the challenges of his own imprisonment to write this wonderful and encouraging book. God gives many wonderful promises in the Bible. Each promise is able to give hope when the prison cells of life close in around us. And like a key, the promises of the Bible open up our prison cells by showing us that things are not as hopeless as they often seem.

God guarantees specific and special blessings to His children. These blessings unlock doors, free captives, and shatter chains that make life a virtual prison sentence. Are you in the dungeon of Doubting Castle? Are you feeling the great blows of the giant called Despair? You have a key to get out! Turn to God's promises. They are "Yes!" in Christ Jesus. The readings and other devotions that follow are just a sample of God's many blessings.

For further study and discussion

Genesis 17:9-22 (vs. 19)
What does God promise Abraham here in this passage? How has God fulfilled His covenantal promises throughout history?

Psalm 89:46-52 (vs. 52)
What promises is the Psalmist recalling here in this chapter? Why does he end the Psalm with praise to God?

Isaiah 43:1-13 (vs. 13)
What promises are given in this passage? How does God reassure us that they will be fulfilled?

Daniel 7:9-18 (vs. 18)
What will the saints of the Most High receive? For how long?

Romans 3:21-31 (vs. 29)
How does God's "yes" provide us comfort in this passage?

Revelation 22:12-21 (vs. 20)
How does this promise encourage us? Does it encourage you?

DAY 14

I Am With You

Reading: Jeremiah 15:10-21 (vs. 20)

One night, a pastor had a dream that greatly discouraged him. In his dream, the minister was standing on top of a huge granite rock formation trying to chip off a piece of it with a pickaxe. Hour after hour, day after day, he worked on the huge rock with no results. He finally gave up, and with desperation, he shouted, "It's useless, I'm wasting my time!"

He threw his axe down and started to walk away from the formation until a stranger approached him. The man said, "Why did you stop? Were you not told to pick at this rock until it chipped off?" The exasperated servant of the Lord responded with a moan, "My work is in vain; I can't even make a single dent in the rock. The task is beyond my ability!"

The stranger gently but firmly answered the minister's resignation by saying: "It should be no concern to you whether the rock yields or not. The work is yours; the results are in the hands of another." And with that bit of encouragement, the minister took up his axe, and with one strike, shattered the rock into a hundred pieces.

In today's reading, Jeremiah feels just like the minister with the axe and the poor results. Jeremiah complains to the Lord that his work was in vain. No one listened to him and everyone hated him because the messages he brought were negative. He tells the Lord that he is in pain, that he is lonely, and that he regrets the day of his birth.

   The Lord responds to Jeremiah in a firm way by telling him to get back to work. But then He reminds the weary prophet of the original promises made to him when he was called to be a prophet: promises to make him like a fortified wall, and to be with him all the way. Isn't it encouraging when we notice in the Bible that the promises of God's continued presence are often given in the context of obedient service? Obedient service is often demanding and appears to yield little fruit from our perspective.

   Jesus gives this final challenge to his church; go into the world, making disciples of all nations, baptizing them, and teaching them truths that they will find hard to believe and obey. But the challenge comes with a Jeremiah-kind of promise; "And surely, I am with you always, to the very end of the age." Be encouraged today as you read and meditate on the passages listed below. God's word reminds us over and over again that we are not alone!

For further study and discussion

Genesis 26:12-25 (vs. 24)
Why was Jacob afraid? How does God's promise bring encouragement to him?

Isaiah 41:1-16 (vs. 10)
What does God's presence mean for those who trust in Him?

Jeremiah 46:25-28 (vs. 28)
What does God's presence guarantee here in this passage?

Haggai 1:12-15 (vs. 13)
What does God's presence mean here in this passage?

Haggai 2:1-8 (vs. 4)
Have you ever experienced the strengthening presence of God in your life?

Matthew 28:16-20 (vs. 20)
How did this promise comfort and encourage the disciples?

DAY 15

Wait!

Reading: Psalm 130 (vs. 5)

Jim Cymbala is the pastor of the Brooklyn Tabernacle in Brooklyn New York. Jim became the pastor of this small urban church when it had a total membership of twenty souls. There were others at first, but many had abandoned ship when the worship services got a little too boring. Consequently, Jim was left with about twenty people and the occasional vagrants who would often wander in from time to time. Jim had doubts about his ministry in Brooklyn and often wondered if he was wasting his time. Jim thought nothing good could come from what he was seeing and from what he was trying to do in the community. Was Jim on a sinking ship that had no future?

On one occasion, Jim needed to meet the mortgage payment for the church building. The mortgage payment was $232 dollars, and the offering that Sunday morning was only $85 dollars. Well, you do the math! And, if you add in the utility bills and even something left over for a pastor's salary, well, let's just say things were not looking up for the Brooklyn Tabernacle!

The mortgage payment was finally due and the church only had $160 in their checking account. Jim was afraid they were going to default on the loan and lose the building. As he was thinking about the possibility of being tossed out on the street, he prayed, "Lord, you have to help me. I don't know much, but I do know that we have to pay this mortgage."*

With a renewed sense of faith, Jim went to the mailbox to check to see if, by chance, someone took pity on them and sent a check. The mail had come, but there was nothing except more bills and a few flyers. Jim was feeling even more defeated until he remembered that the church also had a post office box. "Wait a minute!" Jim said. "Besides the mail slot in the front door, the church also has a post office box. I'll go across the street and see what's there. Surely God will answer my prayer!" But when Jim opened the box, there was no check to be found as he had hoped.

Jim returned back to the office thinking that God had abandoned him. As he unlocked the door, however, he noticed something on the floor that hadn't been there just minutes earlier. It was a plain white envelope without a stamp or any address. Inside, though, there were two $50 bills. Jim shouted out loud with joy, "God, you came through! You came through!"* They now had enough to pay the mortgage. And, to this day, he still doesn't know where that money came from. But, it arrived in the nick of time.

Today, the Brooklyn Tabernacle has a membership numbering in the thousands, and has had a profound impact in the urban area surrounding the church. My friend, look to the Lord today if you feel like you are on a sinking ship. Ask Him for help. And then wait and watch for God's lifeboat to arrive. You may be surprised what, or who, he sends!

For further study and discussion

Exodus 24 (vs. 14)
If you were one of these elders waiting for Moses, what would you be thinking about?

Ruth 3 (vs. 18)
What was Ruth waiting for here in this passage?

Psalm 5 (vs. 3)
Why does the Psalmist give his requests to the Lord in the morning? What does this say about his faith in the Lord?

Acts 1:1-11 (vs. 4)
Why do the disciples have to wait for the Holy Spirit? What are they doing in the "wait-room"?

Titus 2 (vs. 13)
How are we to live while we wait for the Lord's return? What enables us to wait for His return?

Jude 17-23 (vs. 21)
What enables us to wait for Christ's return according to this passage?

DAY 16

Do Not Be Afraid!

Reading: Genesis 15:1-6 (vs. 1)

When your world starts to come unglued, where you do go? Who do you run to? Author Phyllis Ten Elshof says that, when battling the fear of recurrent breast cancer, she first tried to find comfort in statistics:

> "You're gonna be okay," whispered the lady in pink as she wheeled me down the hall, "Eighty percent of breast lumps aren't cancer." I stifled a sigh. So far, statistics had not been in my favor. My breast lump, which was big enough to be seen by the naked eye, hadn't shown up on a mammogram. Mammograms are effective only 80 percent of the time. The volunteer's prediction wasn't accurate, either; I *did* have breast cancer. So why, years after surviving a mastectomy and treatment for breast cancer, was I still drawn to survival statistics like a mosquito to a lamp—especially after hearing that a fellow survivor had recurred? The size of my lump plus five positive nodes drove down my five-year survival rate to less than 25 percent. What's more, I, like so many other cancer survivors, had learned how senseless statistics were in forecasting survival. As one doctor said, "Maybe only 10 percent of patients with your type and stage of cancer are cured, but within that 10 percent, your odds are 0 percent or 100 percent."*

So what drove Phyllis Ten Elshof to statistics? In her book, ***What Cancer Can't Do*** she goes on to say that, "Perhaps it's the kind of fear that drove King Saul to consult a medium on the eve of a battle that would later claim his life (1 Samuel 28). God had stopped communicating with the king through ordinary means, so Saul tried to conjure up the spirit of Samuel to tell him what to do. Saul got the message all right, but it knocked him to the ground."

Phyllis concludes with these thoughts. "Instead of running to statistics (or doctors that quote them) to ease our fears, we should trust in our Heavenly Father, who alone knows how long we will live." God's word for us today echoes her conclusions. Our Lord knows the future and the challenges we will face. Be encouraged that the Lord will certainly be our shield through it all and will fill our hearts with His peace. And, as the passages that follow will remind us, the battles we fight are the Lord's and He will fight through us and for us to His honor and glory.

For further study and discussion

Deuteronomy 1:26-36 (vs. 29)
Why is it comforting to know that God goes before us?

II Chronicles 20:1-17 (vs. 15)
If the battles we often fight are God's, why do we still fear them?
Who preceded the armies (vs. 21)? Why were they given the lead?

Daniel 10 (vs. 12, 19)
What was Daniel doing before the angel delivers his message to
him?

Matthew 28:1-10 (vs. 10)
Why were the women afraid?

Luke 1:26-38 (vs. 30)
Why was Mary afraid? How does the angel comfort her?

John 14:15-27 (vs. 27)
How does the Holy Spirit bring courage and comfort in fearful
times?

DAY 17

Strengthen You!

Reading: Isaiah 40:27-31 (vs. 31)

I think one of the most comforting and encouraging passages in the entire Bible are the words from Isaiah 40, especially the last few verses: **"Though youths grow weary and tired, and vigorous young men stumble badly, yet those who wait for the Lord will gain new strength; they will mount up with wings like eagles, they will run and not get tired, they will walk and not become weary."**

These words brought great comfort to Lisa Beamer, the wife of Todd Beamer, one of the passengers of Flight 93 that crashed in Shanksville, Pennsylvania on 9/11. Lisa was one of many who attended a memorial out in that Shanksville field soon after the crash. There were dignitaries present, including Laura Bush, who spoke words of comfort to the grieving families. But for Lisa, and many of the other families, being there in that field gave them opportunities to leave something of their loved ones behind as a memorial. Lisa left Todd's Chicago Bull's hat, pictures of the family, and a container of M&Ms, Todd's favorite candy.

It was a sunny day in September, and as Lisa was thinking about such a terrible death her husband suffered under the hands of hate-filled people, God brought her comfort. Yes, she knew Todd was with his Lord in heaven. He had built his life and faith upon the firm foundation of Jesus Christ, and he lived out that faith to the very end.

But for Lisa and her children who were left behind, she knew she wasn't going to be left alone. Yes, Todd was with the Lord, but the Lord was with Lisa even on that very difficult day in September. And, as she took one last look at the crash sight, she spotted a hawk soaring high in the sky above the field. A peace flowed over her as God reminded her of the words of Isaiah 40, "Even youths grow tired and weary . . . but those who hope in the Lord will renew their strength. They will soar on wings like eagles."*

Are you tired, discouraged, or lonely? Or, are you grieving the loss of someone close to you today? Those who hope in the Lord will find strength to go on, even to soar like eagles. Be encouraged today, my friend, because God has a special heart for those who are tired, weary, and falling down under the weight of the world.

For further study and discussion

Deuteronomy 3:21-29 (vs. 28)
How does Moses strengthen Joshua?

II Chronicles 16 (vs. 9)
How does the image of God's eyes looking all around encourage us?

Nehemiah 6:1-14 (vs. 9)
Why does Nehemiah pray for strength here in this passage?

Zechariah 10:6-12 (vs. 6, 12)
How has God strengthened you in times of trouble?

I Thessalonians 3:6-13 (vs. 13)
Why does Paul pray for God to strengthen the hearts of the Thessalonians?

II Thessalonians 3:1-5 (vs. 3)
How does God protect us from the evil one?

DAY 18

The Peace of God

Reading: Romans 16:17-20 (vs. 20)

Someone once noticed that you can tell where and when Satan is at work in the world, or in our lives, by adding the prefix "de" or "dis" to any word. For example, Satan has his hand in deception, depression, discouragement, and disappointments. This theory may be a stretch, but we certainly can see Satan's handy work in many areas of life, including another, disharmony.

Satan loves to see discord, disorder, and disloyalty within the life of the church, and, for that matter, all of life. That is why Paul warns the Roman Church in chapter 16 to be aware of false teachers. False teachers were making their rounds within the churches of Asia Minor, and, no doubt, heading towards Rome.

The Roman Church was a "refreshing fellowship", welcoming people into their church, showing hospitality and encouragement to all God sent their way. It is no wonder Paul couldn't wait to meet with these fellow believers after his trip from Jerusalem (Romans 15:31-32). Paul's warning to them at the end of these verses shouldn't come as a surprise. Paul is adding this little post script to encourage them to be discerning. Now there's a "dis" prefix Satan doesn't readily employ!

All of this is an introduction to the words of assurance Paul ends his letter with in the book of Romans. **"The God of Peace will soon crush Satan under your feet."** Yes, Satan brings discord and disbelief into the church and society, but God brings the exact opposite: Peace! When the gospel enters hearts and lives, God's kingdom comes and there is peace. And when the gospel makes inroads into families, and even culture itself, there is peace.

The good news Paul leaves us here in this passage is that Satan's reign of terror is being dismantled as God's kingdom of peace expands in this world. He's even extracting Satan's hold in our own hearts. Are you experiencing one of Satan's attempts to add the prefix "dis" to a word of encouragement in your life today? Remember that God is the God of Peace. No matter what you are up against today, God offers His perfect peace to those whose minds are steadfastly trusting in Him.

For further study and discussion

Numbers 6: 22-27 (vs. 26)
When someone turns his or her face away from you, what does it usually mean? How does the knowledge of the Lord's face turned toward His children bring you peace?

Romans 15:23-33 (vs. 33)
Why does Paul give God this title of peace in this context?

Philippians 4:2-9 (vs. 7, 9)
Have you ever experienced the Lord's transcending peace in your life during a difficult time? How does peace guard our lives?

I Thessalonians 5:12-24 (vs. 23)
How can living a blameless life create peace in our hearts?

II Thessalonians 3:6-18 (vs. 16)
What kind of ways, or in what means, does the Lord give out His peace? In what different ways have you experienced His peace?

Hebrews 13:1-21 (vs. 20)
Why does Paul call the Lord the "God of Peace" here in this passage?

DAY 19

Rescue Me, Lord!

Reading: Romans 7:21-8:2 (vs. 24-25)

A little boy, who had been visiting his grandparents, was given a sling shot. As he was hunting for "big game", he accidentally shot a stone at his grandmother's pet duck and killed it. Johnny quickly hid the duck in a wood pile, but his younger sister Sally had seen the whole thing, and she was determined to use it to her advantage.

After supper the grandmother asked Sally to wash the dishes. But Sally quickly told her grandmother that Johnny wanted to wash the dishes. Before her brother could object, Sally bent over and whispered to him, "I saw you kill the duck, and unless you want me to tell Nanna what you did, you better do what I say." Johnny quickly stepped to the sink and started washing the dishes.

The next day, their grandmother asked Sally to help make lunch. But Sally said, "Johnny wants to help." Once again, she bent over and whispered to Johnny, "Duck." After a few days of doing all of Sally's chores, Johnny couldn't take it any longer and confessed to his grandmother about how he shot and killed her pet duck. But, to Johnny's surprise, his grandmother said, "I know, I was standing at the window and watched you kill Mabel, the duck. I'm glad you came to me and told me about it. I was wondering how long your sister would make a slave of you. And yes, I do forgive you."

Today's theme of encouragement is, "Rescue Me, Lord!" When we think of rescue, our thoughts often turn to enemies who want to do us bodily harm. Or we think about a dangerous place or situation, like a house fire or a disaster that hits the area. Who will quickly forget the people stranded on the rooftops of their homes as the flood waters of Katrina engulfed the city of New Orleans? Many held up signs or spelled out the words "Help us" with pieces of clothes or floating debris.

Like the story of Johnny and Sally, sin and guilt can bully us into thinking that the only way we can be right with God is to become a slave. The Apostle Paul knew all about this kind of slavery as a Pharisee. But as he confesses in Romans 7, the temptation to become a slave to sin or a slave to law in order to "make it up" to God still exists within every Christian. Our sinful natures still desire what is contrary to God's will. But thanks to be God, the Lord Jesus has freed us from the guilt of sin! And, through Jesus Christ, the Spirit of life has rescued us from the law of sin and death.

We will see God's rescuing power and grace in all of the scripture passages that are listed below. But don't forget, as a Christian who has confessed and sought the forgiveness and grace of the Lord, you have been rescued from the guilt and power of sin. Don't let the Sally's or the satanic accusations of the enemy enslave you anymore.

For further study and discussion

Job 5:17-27 (vs. 19)
Who is doing the rescuing here in this passage?

Psalm 72 (vs. 14)
Why does God rescue His children? And from what?

Ezekiel 34:1-16 (vs. 10, 12)
Who does God rescue in this passage? And from whom?

Galatians 1:1-4 (vs. 4)
From what does Jesus rescue us according to Paul here in this passage?

II Timothy 4:9-18 (vs. 18)
What kind, or nature, of attacks does the Lord rescue Paul from here in this passage? How has God rescued you in the past and from what?

II Peter 2:1-10 (vs. 9)
What example does Peter give of God's rescue here in this passage?

DAY 20

The Name of the Lord

Reading: John 14:8-14 (vs. 13)

Not too long ago, a wonderful movie came out in theatres called, "Amazing Grace". It told the life story and work of William Wilberforce of England; a man passionate about ending slavery throughout the British Empire. The movie accurately portrayed the challenges and the many obstacles Wilberforce faced in parliament.

Wilberforce found great encouragement from his friends of the Clapham area and, of course, his old friend John Newton, who penned the words of the song, "Amazing Grace". John Newton had a powerful influence upon Wilberforce as the movie portrayed, because Newton was continually haunted by the thought of his former occupation as a slave ship captain.

But change doesn't come easy especially when money and influence are concerned. It was an uphill battle to pass an abolition law in parliament. In fact, at one point, Wilberforce was ready to give up the fight all together. But then he received a note from an old friend who had influenced the lives of many people in England and the world over, John Wesley, the founder of Methodism. He heard of Wilberforce's discouragement and wrote the following note to Wilberforce just before the old revivalist died:

"Unless God has raised you up for this very thing, you will be worn out by the opposition of men and devils.

**But if God be for you, who can be against you? Are all of
them stronger than God?"**

John Wesley died six days later, but Wilberforce went on with
renewed courage to win the battle over slavery and other pressing
issues facing the British Empire. He was able to lead and move the
British Parliament with fervency, and even faith, because he was
doing it all for the name of the Lord Jesus and His kingdom.

Are you discouraged today and feeling like your fighting a
losing battle all by yourself? Think again, my friend! Take these
same words John Wesley gave to William Wilberforce and apply
them to your own life today. Unless God has raised you for this very
challenge, you are going to wear yourself out with discouragement
and despair. If God has given you specific responsibilities and
has called you to care for an ill spouse, lead a group of people in
some kind of ministry, or even lead the charge to stop injustice, be
assured that he will give you exactly what you need every day. Take
the words of John 14:13 & 14 to heart about prayer and kingdom
work. Challenge yourself with these words of encouragement: **"Are
all of your struggles stronger than God?"**

For further study and discussion

Genesis 13:1-4 (vs. 4)
What did it mean for Abram to call upon the name of the Lord?

Psalm 20 (vs. 7)
Do you often find yourself trusting in 21st century chariots and horses instead of the Lord?

Psalm 116 (vs. 4, 17)
How did the Psalmist call upon the name of the Lord?

Isaiah 50 (vs. 10)
How does Isaiah describe people who do not trust in the name of the Lord?

Joel 2:28-32 (vs. 32)
What power does the name of the Lord have according to this passage?

James 5:7-18 (vs. 14)
What does it mean to pray "in the name of the Lord?"

DAY 21

How much more . . . ?

Reading: Luke 12:24-28 (vs. 24)

Are you anxious about something today? You can't sleep at night because you're worrying about something that has happened or is about to happen. Or, you're creating all sorts of negative scenarios in your mind based more on fiction than truth. Sound familiar? I can assure you, you're not alone! We live in an anxious time; threats of terrorism, prices for gas going through the roof, and concerns about the environment. It's easy to see why we live with anxiety and fear of what tomorrow may bring.

Martin Luther, the father of the Lutheran Church and a former Catholic monk, had a problem with excessive worry and anxiety during a critical point in his life. In fact, Luther was down right depressed. Here was one of the great reformers of the Church; a man who nailed the 95 thesis onto the door of the Wittenberg Castle in Germany, a man who was a Bible scholar and theologian, having taught and wrote a great many things about God's love and care for His people, was living with a bout of anxiety. It was a-typical for Luther to be so down. He wasn't known for being a man with clinical depression. But on this occasion, something was worrying the man to a point that he wasn't sleeping, eating, or socializing with others.

In fact, his anxiety had so darkened his outlook on life, that his wife Katherine took the matter into her own hands. Something had to be done to snap Martin Luther out of his depression! Katherine came down with dark funeral clothes on, looking the part of a mourner. Luther asked his wife, "Who died?" His wife said, "I have cause for the saddest of weeping for God in heaven has died." Luther shot back, "God has not died!" She came back with this rebuke, "Well then, live like it and act like it!" Needless to say, Luther was chided for his dreadful fear and excessive worry. Someone put the whole incident to verse, finishing the poem with these words:

> **"Her gentle rebuke did not fail him, He laughingly kissed his wise spouse, took courage, and banished his sorrow, and joy again reigned in the house."**

Are you living today as if God were dead? Do you feel like God isn't in control of this world, or your world? Do you wonder if God really cares about you or if God has just left you alone? Jesus told his disciples not to worry about the things of this world. God not only feeds the birds of the air, but also clothes the lilies of the field with His own hands. Are you not more valuable than birds and plants? Why wouldn't He look after you and provide you with all that you need? Besides, there are enough concerns for one day and no need to borrow tomorrow's concerns.

Let me encourage you today to write out on a piece of paper all of the things that are troubling you. And then, one by one, ask the Lord to deal with each of your issues or concerns through prayer. Finish your prayer time by tossing your list away.

For further study and discussion

Song of Solomon 4:8-15 (vs. 10)
What does the "how much more . . ." statement refer to in this passage?

Matthew 7:7-12 (vs. 11)
What is the prerequisite of God's "how much more . . ." gift-giving?

Matthew 12:1-14 (vs. 12)
What does the "how much more . . ." statement refer to in this passage?

Romans 5:1-11 (vs. 9, 15)
What does the "how much more . . ." statement communicate about God's grace?

I Corinthians 6:1-11 (vs. 3)
What does the "how much more . . ." statement encourage the Corinthians to do, or not to do?

Hebrews 9:11-15 (vs. 14)
How does the "how much more . . ." statement encourage Christians here in this passage?

DAY 22

New Life!

Reading: II Corinthians 5:11-21 (vs. 17)

One of C.S. Lewis's classic Narnia books is entitled, "*The Voyage of the Dawn Treader.*" In this story, Lewis has incorporated only two of the Pevensie children, Edmund and Lucy. In addition to Edmund and Lucy, we meet a relative of the children who is also drawn into the land of Narnia. He is their cousin, Eustace Scrubb, a very spoiled and miserable kid. But while the children travel in Narnia, Eustace Scrubb becomes a hideous dragon because he had stolen a golden arm piece. His own greed turns him into a dragon.

The children finally meet up with Aslan, the Lion who is King of Narnia. They follow Aslan to a very high mountain where there is a well for Eustace to bathe his aching dragon feet. But in order for him to get into the water, he needs to undress. Now Eustace thought it odd that he, as a dragon, had to undress. Dragon's don't wear clothes, he thought.

But Aslan meant something totally different. Eustace began to understand that Dragons are like snakes, needing to shed old skin. So Eustace starts to scratch off the old scales of his dragon skin until all of the dragon skin falls off. But underneath the old skin he sees that his skin is still rough and scaly. So he starts to scratch his skin again, only to find another rough dragon skin underneath.

Finally, Aslan says to Eustace, "You have to let me undress you!"* So the lion takes his claws and begins to tear into the dragon skin with painful and deep blows. Surely death will follow, the boy thinks to himself. But, soon, the gnarled mess of dragon skin is cut away, and the boy is thrown into the cool water where he comes out a young boy again.

Lewis writes this story to illustrate the characteristics of joy. Eustace Scrubb sees what his inner life of greed and rotten behavior is like through the skin and scales of the dragon. The dragon inside becomes the dragon on the outside as well. The only hope for his restoration is by surrendering his life into the hands, or shall I say, the claws of Aslan the Lion King. With the deep and painful work of Aslan scratching away the old skin, a new creation emerges and is able to bathe in the waters. This is a different undressing then we are used to.

Joy comes when we, too, surrender to the Lord of Life. Sometimes our discouragement and joylessness comes from hearts that are becoming "dragon like." If that describes you today, then go to Christ and ask him to peel away that old dragon's heart, and claw away all the old scales of selfishness. You can't do it on your own; it takes a trained surgeon with very sharp claws like Aslan. But, be encouraged, when the Lord finishes his work in your life, you will experience the refreshing and joy-filled waters of new life.

For further study and discussion

Ezra 9:5-15 (vs. 9)
What is the "new life" that Ezra prays about here in this passage?

John 3:1-8 (vs. 3, 7)
How do we receive "new life" according to this passage? Have you received this new life?

Romans 6:1-14 (vs. 4)
How does baptism represent "new life" in Christ?

II Corinthians 4:7-18 (vs. 16)
What does Paul mean when he tells us we are outwardly wasting away?

Colossians 3:1-17 (vs. 10)
How does knowledge bring renewal in our spiritual lives?

I Peter 1:13-25 (vs. 23)
What is the imperishable seed Peter describes here in this passage? How does this fact encourage suffering Christians?

DAY 23

You will be called . . .

Reading: Philippians 2:12-18 (vs. 15)

In his book entitled, "The Rise of Christianity", Rodney Stark documents a time in the early Christian church when the conversion rate was 40% per decade. The first three centuries of the Christian church grew despite persecutions, divisions, and limited exposure. How did the early church grow so fast? One of the reasons for this growth, according to Stark, was the way Christians loved each other, and even those outside of the church.

He gives an example of the power of God's love, demonstrated through the early church. The Roman Empire faced one of its greatest challenges in the year 251 A.D. It wasn't from an outside army, but rather an inside army. A measles epidemic claimed millions of lives in the Roman Empire, with whole cities wiped out. In fact, there are some estimates that one third of the population of the Roman Empire died that year.

But how did this contribute to the growth of the church? The Christians living in the Roman Empire cared for their own sick families and friends when they contracted measles. In contrast, their neighbors, who were not Christians, would push their own family members out onto the streets to live and die alone at the first signs of measles. The Christians, at great risk to their own lives, went out onto the streets and helped many of these sick and dying people who were abandoned by their own family members. When the epidemic was over, the love of these Christians so moved people in the Roman Empire, many who weren't Christians became

Christians. In fact, the Roman Emperor said of these Christians, "They shine like stars."

Maybe you can't preach a sermon and stand before huge crowds like Billy Graham, or you can't write powerful, moving books like C.S. Lewis, challenging the hearts and minds of people intellectually; but if you love with courage and persistence, you showcase God's love and power to the people around you. And the people around you do take notice. If a pagan Roman emperor stood up and took note of Christ's love through the church, so will your friends, neighbors, and co-workers.

Be encouraged with the words of Jesus from his Sermon on the Mount: "Let your light shine before men, that they may see your good deeds and praise your Father in heaven." Live who you are as God's children.

For further study and discussion

Isaiah 1:18-31 (vs. 26)
When will the city be called "the City of Righteousness" and "the Faithful City"?

Isaiah 56:1-8 (vs. 5)
Who is the "memorial" for in this passage? What is your "memorial"?

Isaiah 58:6-14 (vs. 12)
What will the people in this passage be called? And for what reason?

Isaiah 61:1-7 (vs. 3, 6)
What would it mean for the Jews to be called "priests"? What does it mean today for Christians (see I Peter 2)?

Isaiah 62: 1-5 (vs. 2)
What does it mean to be called "a new name"? Why would anyone desire to be called by "another name"?

Isaiah 62: 6-12 (vs. 12)
What new names are given to God's people here in this passage? Are Christians called these names today? How so?

DAY 24

Never the less . . .

Reading: Jeremiah 33:1-9 (vs. 6)

There is a famous Spanish story about reconciliation and forgiveness. Whether the story is actually true or not doesn't matter because the message of the story is telling. In the story, a father and son became estranged. Some disagreement or issue got blown out of proportion so the son left home for good. The father later set out to find his son in order to make up with his son, but his son was no where to be found. He searched for months with no success. Finally, out of desperation he placed an ad in a newspaper. His ad simply read: "Dear Paco, meet me in front of this newspaper office at noon on Saturday. All is forgiven. I love you. Your Father."

On Saturday, eight hundred young men by the name of Paco showed up looking for forgiveness and love from their estranged fathers. We don't now if one of the 800 Pacos who showed up that Saturday was the Paco who was asked to show up, but we can be assured that there was one father waiting among the many estranged sons for his own son to return.

This story should remind us of the parable Jesus told about the prodigal son. Here was a kid who offended his father, took his inheritance, and blew the whole wad on himself. When he finally decides to return, thinking reconciliation with his father impossible, he returns to his father's house to become a slave. Oh, wasn't he surprised when he returned home!

The way Jesus tells the story makes us think about how much God the Father wants us to be reconciled to Him. The Father in the story sees his fallen son from a distance and then he runs to meet him. Older Jewish men don't run, they walk. It's not dignified for Jewish men to run. But this Father doesn't care, and for that matter, neither did the father in our Paco story. All that matters is reconciliation to a father.

Beyond the Paco story, and behind the parable that Jesus told, is a message of reconciliation. God's "nevertheless" is an adverb that speaks of grace. In spite of what we've done or have become, God remains the same and His promises are sure. Regardless of the past, God offers a much better future in His household.

For further study and discussion

II Samuel 5:1-10 (vs. 7)
What was David's experience of God's "never the less . . ." here in this passage?

II Chronicles 21:4-7 (vs. 7)
What does the "never the less . . ." phrase here in this passage tell us about God's grace and promises?

Job 17 (vs. 9)
What is the message of the "never the less . . ." phrase here in this passage?

Isaiah 9: 1-7 (vs. 1)
The "never the less . . ." phrase connects chapter 9 to the previous chapter. Why? What is the message of encouragement found in chapter 9?

Acts 5:12-16 (vs. 14)
How does the "never the less . . ." phrase in this passage encourage Christians today? How does it encourage the persecuted church?

II Timothy 2:14-26 (vs. 19)
How did the "never the less . . ." phrase help to encourage young Pastor Timothy here in this passage?

DAY 26

Bread for His Children

Reading: I Thessalonians 5:12-24 (vs. 18)

The Apostle Paul writes in I Thessalonians 5:18 "**. . . in everything give thanks; for this is God's will for you in Christ Jesus.**" You might be thinking to yourself, "Easy for you to say. How I can be thankful to God with the stuff I'm dealing with right now? How can these difficulties even be God's will?" That's exactly how Corrie Ten Boom felt back in the days when she and her sister, Betsy, were held against their will in a Nazi concentration camp.

Corrie's book, entitled "The Hiding Place", tells about her family's experiences of hiding Jews in their Dutch home during World War II. The Ten Boom's were betrayed by a Nazi sympathizer and were arrested for their crime. Corrie and Betsy were sent to the Ravensbruck Concentration Camp. Like all of the other Nazi death camps, this one was full of brutal guards and death. The camp also had its share of fleas.

In the crowded and flea infested barracks that the Ten Boom sisters called home, it was difficult to give thanks. In fact, one morning they read the same verse from I Thessalonians 5, quoted above, about giving thanks in all circumstances. Betsy told the ladies who were reading and studying this passage that they had to give thanks for their barracks, and even for the fleas in the barracks. Corrie snapped and said, "No way am I going to give thanks to God for these dreadful fleas!"* But Betsy was persuasive and eventually they bowed their heads and gave thanks to God for even the fleas.

As the months went on in that dreadful camp, the guards became more brutal and cracked down heavily on groups gathering for prayer and Bible study. Barracks inspections were a daily occurrence for most of the camp except for the barracks the Ten Booms shared. In fact, their barracks was left relatively free so they could do Bible studies, talk openly, and even pray in their barracks. It was truly a refuge for the ladies in this dark and evil place.

Come to find out, the reason why the guards avoided their barracks, allowing the ladies the freedom they had was due to the fleas! Their barracks had all the fleas and the fleas made all the difference. You might say God created those pesky fleas and permitted them to "bug" the ladies so they could enjoy something even greater . . . freedom and protection from evil.

As our heavenly Father, He knows what we need in each and every circumstance. He may withhold luxuries and extravagant accommodations, but never the things we need and even the things that are "good" for us. God's promise to us is that everything works for the good of those who love Him and are called according to His purposes.

For further study and discussion

I Kings 17:1-6 (vs. 6)
Have you ever experienced God's miraculous provision in your life? Has there ever been a time in your life when you had a deep need? How did God provide for your need?

I Kings 17: 7-16 (vs. 13)
What does this passage say about tithes and offerings to the Lord? Why did she have to feed Elijah first?

Psalm 37:16-26 (vs. 25)
What is at stake (not the food) here in this promise?

Psalm 78: 17-31 (vs. 25)
Why does the Psalmist call the manna in the wilderness the "bread of Angels"?

Matthew 6:9-13 (vs. 11)
Why does Jesus teach us to pray for our daily bread when the Lord already knows we need food to survive?

John 6:25-33 (vs. 32)
What is the "true bread" Jesus is talking about here in this passage? How does this bread satisfy our hunger?

Day 27

It's Morning Again!

Reading: Psalm 30 (vs. 5)

Perhaps you remember the presidential campaign of 1980 when Ronald Reagan ran against President Jimmy Carter for the White House. President Carter faced many uphill battles during his term as president following the campaign, which included a gas shortage, inflation, and the Iran hostage crisis.

I remember those long lines at the gas stations and the huge interest rates that left people with little extra money to buy things outside of the necessities of life. Add to these the fear of nuclear war and the helplessness of the United States to rescue our own citizens held hostage in Iran, and you have the ingredients for a cranky and pessimistic citizenry.

But an effective campaign advertisement from the Reagan campaign team illustrated that things would change if Ronald Reagan became president. The ad was called, "It's Morning Again in America", and it featured a morning sunrise with promises that, under Ronald Reagan, our dark night of suffering would soon give way to a morning of hope and optimism for the future. The ad worked because Ronald Reagan became the 40th president of the United States.

The hopeful and optimistic picture of a bright new day is a biblical theme that has brought encouragement to people throughout the ages. In the context of our reading from Psalm 30 today, David is rejoicing at the dedication of the temple. He is an old man at this time and soon his son, Solomon, will assume the throne and build the temple. David had his share of dark days; the threat of King Saul, the threat of the Philistines, the terrible day when the Ark didn't arrive in Jerusalem and Uzzah died, the period of sin and guilt after he stole another man's wife and lost a child, and the very dark days of being a parent with a son like Absolam. David knew what it was like to wear sackcloth and cry one-self to sleep at night.

But David's encouragement for us is that weeping may last for a night, but because we belong to the Lord, the morning will come and it will bring rejoicing and dancing. If you don't believe David, just ask the ladies, especially Mary who found an empty tomb and a risen savior in the morning.

For further study and discussion

Job 11:7-20 (vs. 17)
What will morning bring according to this passage?

Psalm 5 (vs. 3)
What should we be doing in the morning according to this passage?
Why the morning?

Psalm 46 (vs. 5)
Why is the Psalmist so sure that victory will come in the morning?

Psalm 59 (vs. 16)
Why will the Psalmist sing songs of victory in the morning?

Lamentations 3:1-24 (vs. 23)
What kept Jeremiah encouraged during this awful time when Jerusalem was under siege by an enemy, and misery was all around him inside the city?

Mark 16:1-8 (vs. 1-2)
How does the early morning discovery of an empty tomb give us hope today?

DAY 28

Light

Reading: Psalm 27 (vs. 1)

Author J. R. R. Tolkien became a household name after the three-part movie series entitled, "Lord of the Rings". Because man was not able to rid himself of the "precious": a powerful ring which both entices and destroys the bearer of it, Middle Earth is being insidiously overrun by the forces of evil. It was a powerful and addictive temptation, placing the entire Middle Earth in jeopardy.

The only hope for the salvation of Middle Earth is a hobbit that volunteers to take the ring back to the mountain where it was formed, and subsequently destroy it. But evil doesn't give up, as both the book and the movie vividly portray. Evil corrupts those who were thought to be friends and allies, dividing in order to conquer.

One of my favorite episodes happens in the second movie when the race of men and elves get boxed-in at Helmsdeep, a mountain fortress. The white wizard, Solrun, has joined forces with Morador, forming an army of ugly, evil, and destructive beasts. They march against the rag tag group of men and elves hunkered down in that mountain fortress. As the battle grows more intense and they realize they are outmanned and outgunned, the men and the elves begin to run out of hope.

But then, in the morning of the third day, Gandolf the White comes with reinforcements. As Gandolf approaches, he shines a bright light that blinds the eyes of the evil beasts. Just in the nick of time, the light of the morning sun shines with reinforcements. This episode ends with victory. But there are more battles to fight until the final decisive battle at the end of the series.

Tolkien writes his stories as a Christian, illustrating Christian truths through these characters and plots. In this episode, a major victory is won which enables Middle Earth to have hope and opportunity to finally defeat evil in the end. That fits with what Tolkien believed and put into words through a letter he wrote to a friend:

> **"No man can estimate what is really happening at the present. All we do know, and that to a large extent by direct experience, is that evil labors with vast power and perpetual success . . . but ultimately in vain . . . preparing always only the soil for unexpected good to sprout in."***

The next time you see an eye full of evil, remember that it will have its day of reckoning. In fact, the light is shining even now through God's word. As God's children, we can be assured that dawn is about to break. And at the end, darkness and gloom will be totally eliminated in the new heaven and earth. We will bask in the light of God's glory forever.

For further study and discussion

II Samuel 23:1-7 (vs. 4)
Who is David describing in verse 4? How does this description fit Jesus?

Psalm 4 (vs. 6)
What does it mean for God to shine His face upon us?

Daniel 2:19-23 (vs. 22)
How does light dwell with the Lord? What does that mean here in this passage?

John 1:1-9 (vs. 4)
Why do people reject the Light of the world?

II Corinthians 4:1-13 (vs. 6)
How does the Lord shine His light in our hearts? What becomes visible through this light?

Revelation 22:1-5 (vs. 5)
What will give us light in the new heavens and earth? Why is this light a comforting hope for Christians?

DAY 29

Wings

Reading: Psalm 36 (vs. 7)

Psalm 36 is a record of extremes. It's an example of the depths of man's fallen heart. But it's also a record of the height of God's love and mercy. It seems almost ridiculous to bring these two subjects together under one Psalm, but the Psalmist does so in order to highlight his suffering and his ultimate security.

Living in this fallen world, all of us face suffering and heartache. Perhaps today you suffer because you're living the Christian life among people who are doing everything in their power to tempt or discourage you in your faith. Or, perhaps today your heart aches because someone abused you or proved unfaithful to you. And, in this fallen world, we are constantly being reminded of our own weaknesses and our own mortality. Yes, the trials we face are enough to make us curl up in a fetal position and cry like a child.

But David, the author of this Psalm, finds comfort in the image of hiding under the shadow of God's wings. Like a helpless baby bird tucked away in a nest within the watchful protection of its mother, there is also assurance for God's children. As we wait and come near to Him, we find true rest under His wings.

Pastor Cleland McAfee was pasturing a church in 1901 when he received devastating news that his two nieces had died of diphtheria. He was very close to the two sisters and the grief was intense. But, as he turned to God for comfort, he experienced the nearness of God and His sustaining peace. Pastor McAfee's heart was filled with comfort and assurance. It was this peace that inspired him to write a poem that has brought peace to countless others throughout the years.

In fact, Pastor McAfee stood with his choir outside the quarantined home of his brother on the day of the funeral, singing the words of this poem, encouraging those who attended to find their refuge in the shadow of God's wings.

> *"There is a place of quiet rest, near to the heart of God, a place where sin cannot molest, near to the heart of God. There is a place of comfort sweet, near to the heart of God, a place where we our savior meet, near to the heart of God. There is a place of full release, near to the heart of God, a place where all is joy and peace, near to the heart of God. O Jesus blest redeemer, sent from the heart of God, hold us who wait before Thee, near to the heart of God."*

For further study and discussion

Psalm 17 (vs. 8)
Why does David find comfort in the shadow of God's wings? What trial was he experiencing according to verses 9-14?

Psalm 57 (vs. 1)
Read I Samuel 24 and then read the Psalm once again. How did David's disaster pass?

Psalm 63 (vs. 7)
Read I Samuel 27 and then read the Psalm once again. How does David endure this fearful time in his life?

Psalm 91 (vs. 4)
According to this Psalm, why does David find refuge under God's wings?

Isaiah 40:25-31 (vs. 31)
What comforting message does this "winged" image give tired Christians?

Malachi 4:1-3 (vs. 2)
How do wings bring healing according to this passage?

DAY 30

Shepherd

Reading: John 10:11-21 (vs. 11)

It's a humbling thing to be considered as sheep in need of a shepherd. Although, from our 21st century stand point, being considered a member of a particular church "flock" isn't offensive. In fact, people often find strength in numbers. However, true courage doesn't come from safety in numbers, but from the Shepherd of the flock.

Sheep have no natural defenses; they're not fast, they don't have sharp teeth or claws, they don't have camouflage, they aren't very smart, and they really don't have strength in numbers. If one sheep jumps over an imaginary object, the rest of the flock will follow the lead and jump over the same imaginary obstacle. In fact, entire flocks of sheep have been known to jump over cliffs to their deaths because they're not creatures of discernment.

It seems as if God made sheep just this way so that they would have a symbiotic relationship with man. They are completely dependent upon the shepherd to protect them, lead them, and even feed and water them. The shepherd of Psalm 23 leads the flock of sheep to green pastures and coaxes them to drink by bringing them near quiet ponds of water. Sheep don't like water, especially the fast moving river water, but they need to drink. Wool coats make for poor diving suits!

Throughout the Bible, we see this theme of shepherd and sheep used in a special way to highlight God's gracious and wise care over His children. The only time we see shepherds viewed in negative ways are when God's under-shepherds (kings, priests, prophets, leaders, elders, pastors, etc.) abuse and mistreat His sheep. That is why Jesus tells his disciples that he is the "Good Shepherd". Jesus is the very embodiment of shepherding love and care. Unlike the hired hands, that care nothing about the flock, Jesus lays down his life for His sheep.

Jesus is the shepherd who even goes after lost lambs, like the one lost lamb in the parable found in Luke 15. When sheep get lost from the flock, they become bewildered and simply plop down where they are at, not willing to move an inch. They won't even move when they see the shepherd come after them! The shepherd is forced to carry the lost lamb back to the fold. What a beautiful, and yet accurate, picture of our Shepherd's love for us, His sheep. Be encouraged today or through the week as you read more about our Shepherd's gracious love.

For further study and discussion

Genesis 49:22-26 (vs. 24)
How is the Shepherd described here in this verse?

Psalm 23 (vs. 1)
How has this Psalm comforted you in the past?

Psalm 28 (vs. 9)
How does God carry the nation of Israel throughout her history?

Isaiah 40:6-11 (vs. 11)
How does this picture of God's tender care for lambs and ewes comfort you today?

Hebrews 13:11-21 (vs. 20)
Who is the Great Shepherd of the sheep? How does this shepherd equip us?

Revelation 7:9-17 (vs. 17)
Jesus is pictured here as both lamb and shepherd. What message does this picture convey about the love of Christ?

Day 31

Rocks, Stones, and Fortresses

Reading: Psalm 46 (vs. 7, 11)

In C. S. Lewis's children's series, "The Chronicles of Narnia", young heroine Lucy meets a majestic lion named Aslan in the enchanted land of Narnia. Making a return visit a year later, the children discover that everything has changed radically, and they quickly become lost. But, after a series of dreadful events, Lucy finally spots Aslan in a forest clearing. She rushes to him, throws her arms around his neck, and buries her face in his mane.

> **"Welcome child," he said.**
> **"Aslan," said Lucy, "you're bigger."**
> **"That's because you're older, little one," answered he.**
> **"I'm not. But each year you grow, you'll find me bigger."***

Everything in our world is in flux. As we grow older, our appearance changes and even our attitudes and tastes often change. Hopefully we grow wiser as we grow older, if we can remember. Our neighborhoods change. Our world gets smaller. And, in the course of all of these changes, we lose friends and family members. Kids move out and move away from home. Death leaves empty and aching spots in our lives.

All of this change scares us, especially with the accelerated pace of it in the past thirty years. But there is one constant that never changes. God's people have found comfort and strength, knowing that God is the one constant in our lives. God cannot, nor will

He ever, change in character or alter what He has promised. He is our rock and fortress even when the earth gives way and the mountains fall into the heart of the sea. And when wars break out and trouble surrounds us on every side, the Lord's love and care for us will never diminish. He is the one who breaks the bow and shatters the spear!

It's been suggested by scholars that Psalm 46 was written after the King of Assyria taunted King Hezekiah and the people of Jerusalem while under siege. **"Now therefore do not let Hezekiah deceive you or mislead you like this, and do not believe him, for no god of any nation or kingdom was able to deliver his people from my hand or from the hand of my fathers . . ."** (II Chron.32:15).

Hezekiah did not cower under the threat of this bully. Neither did David when facing another taunting enemy of his own. Both men found God to be larger than their enemies. We will, too, when we become still, surrendering our troubles to the Rock of the Ages. The more we mature in faith, the larger Christ becomes in our eyes and in our hearts.

For further study and discussion

Psalm 18:1-3 (vs. 2)
What enemies has God delivered you from in the past several years?

Psalm 31 (vs. 2, 3)
On what basis does the Psalmist call for God's help as a refuge?

Psalm 62 (vs. 2, 6)
What image comes to your mind when you think of rocks and fortresses? What does David mean when he says that he "will not be shaken"?

Daniel 2:24-45 (vs. 44-45)
Who is the "Rock" described here in this passage? How is this "rocky" image used to bring comfort unto God's people?

Matthew 21:33-46 (vs. 42)
Who is the "rejected" stone referring to in this passage? What's the importance of a cornerstone?

I Peter 2:4-8 (vs. 8)
How or why does Jesus make people stumble and fall?

DAY 32

God's Chariots Are Coming!

Reading: Psalm 68:1-17 (vs. 17)

This Psalm was used during the Feast of Weeks or in tabernacles as the Israelites celebrated God's provision after the harvest. It is a Psalm that lifts the emotions to a fevered pitch, celebrating God's power in the defense, protection, and provision of His people.

It has long been thought that David wrote Psalm 68. It is believed that David wrote the Psalm as the Ark was brought into the center of the city of Jerusalem. David rejoices in the fact that God brought His children up out of bondage from Egypt, establishing them in the land with Zion as the capitol. The journey from Egypt to Jerusalem took centuries, and against all odds, humanly speaking.

David's own experience against the Philistines filled this Psalm with worship and heart-felt assurance of God's power. Through God's power, he was able to bring down Goliath. And when the ill-equipped army of Israel went to battle against the ironclad warriors of Philistia, David was told to wait until he heard the marching sounds of God's army on top of the balsam trees. God's army marched ahead of David's puny little army to win the day. (II Sam. 5)

We can find great courage today when we consider God's huge arsenal. Of course, we don't use chariots and horsemen to fight military conflicts today, but His army is still the most lethal this world will ever see. Elisha tells us that, "Those who are with us are more than those who are with them. (II Kings 6)" Hell itself can throw all it has against God's people, and it still isn't enough to defeat God's army encamped around His children!

As David pictures God as victorious and seated in His capitol, and surrounded by his heavenly host, we, too, should see the ascended and victorious Jesus sitting on the throne. His ascension enables us to have the same kind of confidence that both David and Elisha had when they were up against innumerable odds. Christ made a public spectacle of the demonic host (Colossians 3:15) through his death and resurrection. And he continues to give us the victory by equipping us with spiritual gifts.

Don't ever feel outnumbered in this world! The enemies of the Lord flee and scatter in the sight of God's armies. And when you feel surrounded by the enemy, don't forget to look at who surrounds your enemies!

For further study and discussion

II Samuel 5:17-25 (vs. 24)
Do you believe the Lord goes out "in front of you" as a Christian when you face enemies and major challenges? If so, how has it changed the way you viewed these challenges?

II Kings 2:1-14 (vs. 12)
How did the fire, horses, and chariots encourage Elisha when his friend and mentor left him?

II Kings 6:8-23 (vs. 17)
If the Lord were to open our eyes today, would we see the same spiritual army surrounding us (see Psalm 68:17)?

Psalm 20 (vs. 7)
Do you trust the Lord in, and for, all things? If not, what are your "chariots" and "horses"?

Jeremiah 4:5-13 (vs. 13)
Why does Jeremiah compare God's chariots to a whirlwind and His horses to eagles? How should these images comfort us in our times of trouble?

Colossians 2:6-15 (vs. 15)
Who are the powers and authorities in this verse? How did Jesus make a public spectacle of them?

DAY 33

Raise up a Banner!

Reading: Exodus 17:8-16 (vs. 15)

The Amalekites were a notorious band of pillagers, rapists, and cruel bandits. This group preyed particularly upon those lagging behind the company of Israel as they marched through the desert. The weary and sick, the old and the children, were often kept to the back of this huge caravan. The actions of these desperados were seen by God to be the very embodiment of evil. It's no wonder God wanted the memory of these people to be blotted out!

But the way God chooses to fight this evil is interesting, and a bit perplexing. Why is Moses called to raise his staff during the battle? And why does the army lose the moment Moses' arms grow tired? The answer is found in the name of the alter God instructs Moses to build after the battle: "The Lord is my banner."

The Hebrew word translated for "banner" is *nissi*. It is a word used in other Old Testament passages to mean pole, sail, or flag. But here, in this passage, the banner seems to be Moses' staff: The same staff that was raised before Pharaoh and the Egyptians during the plagues and the Red Sea victory. Consider the staff to be God's flag that rallies the army to fight in war. But, in this case, it means more than just a symbol to rally the troops; it's a reminder that the Lord is the only one who can bring victory. The people needed to be reminded of that, and God wanted Joshua to be reminded of it as well. Joshua will eventually be called to lead the people against new threats in the promised-land. God also wants us to be reminded that he is our Jehovah-*nissi*.

Sometimes we grow tired of waiting upon God for victories, don't we? We think it's easier to fight battles with our own power and with our own ingenuity than to seek out God's wisdom and strength against evil. But rallying around God's banner, and trusting *in* God *as* "our banner", can easily be two different things. If the Lord is worthy of your loyalty, He should also be worthy of your trust. Like the Amalekites of old, evil is not to be taken lightly. Be assured, though, that God desires a decisive victory in your life, and He is able to bring this about as Jehovah-*nissi*.

For further study and discussion

Psalm 60 (vs. 4)
Where is this banner to be "unfurled" according to verse 4? Why
would anyone unfurl a banner against a bow?

Song of Solomon 2:3-13 (vs. 4)
How does the Lord raise a banner of love over us? How has he
raised a banner of love over you in your life?

Isaiah 11:10-16 (vs. 12)
When God raises a banner for the nations, whose picture will be
on that banner according to verse 11?

Isaiah 18 (vs. 3)
Is this a picture of Christ's return? If so, how does it encourage us
as Christians to live our lives when facing trials and opposition?

Isaiah 49:22-26 (vs. 22)
Why does God lift up His banner to the peoples of the world?
What message will this banner communicate to the world?

Jeremiah 50:1-10 (vs. 2)
The banner that Jeremiah speaks of in this passage declares victory
over Babylon. How is this message of victory similar to the one
given in Revelation 18?

DAY 34

Reward

Reading: Galatians 6:6-10 (vs. 9)

The Apostle Paul often uses agricultural metaphors in his letters and especially here in Galatians with his references to *seed, fruit of the Spirit, reaping, sowing, and harvest*. It makes sense Paul used terms related to farming since most of the people of his time had an agrarian background.

Additionally, the analogies of sowing, growing, and reaping are most helpful in describing the dynamics of the spiritual life. Seeds need to be planted before there can be any harvest. And before there can be fruitful harvest, the farmer has to care for the plants through pruning, cultivating, watering, and weeding.

The farmer does a lot of work throughout the growing season. But when he sows seed in the spring time, he really doesn't know whether the plants will grow, survive, or garner a fair price at the end. Farming is a speculative adventure because there are no guarantees in nature.

Sometimes we get discouraged serving the Lord and helping others because we view it as a "speculative" adventure. Quite often, we wonder if we are wasting our time and talents with people who show so little growth. Or, we remember a past situation when we served the Lord with great idealism and passion, only to find that our work was in vain. Perhaps you've spent considerable time helping out a young person who had a rough start in life, but as time went on, you could see that he or she wasn't appreciative. And, from your point of view, the spiritual seed never germinated.

Paul says to us in today's passage, "Spiritual farming comes with a guarantee." It is never a speculative adventure! We can be encouraged today and this week, as we read and meditate upon God's word. God does not forget our work, and neither will we when see for ourselves the treasures stored up in heaven!

Edward Kimball was a hard working shoe shop assistant and faithful Sunday-school teacher. He daily prayed for the kids in his classes and spent hours discipling them in the Word. One of his students became the famous evangelist, D.L. Moody. Moody, in turn, preached to thousands of people in his lifetime. One of Moody's converts was F.B. Meyer who became a popular preacher and Bible teacher. Meyer, in turn, was used by God to lead J.W. Chapman to the faith. God used Chapman to bring the famous baseball player, Billy Sunday, to Christ. Sunday, in turn, became an evangelist and had a great impact upon another young man by the name of Mordecai Ham. And, it was during an evangelistic rally in Charlotte North Carolina where Mordecai Ham preached to a young Billy Graham. Edward Kimball had no idea his work with a young boy would be used in such a way. What a wonderful reward for obedience and faithful service!

For further study and discussion

Psalm 62 (vs. 12)
On what basis can we be assured that our work for the Lord will be rewarded?

Isaiah 62 (vs. 11)
Who brings the reward according to this verse? What, or who, might be the "recompense" that accompanies him?

Matthew 5:11-16 (vs. 12)
What kind of reward awaits the persecuted? Who are the "persecuted" according to verses 11 and 12?

Matthew 6:1-21 (vs. 6, 4, 18)
What kind of reward awaits those who give, pray, and fast anonymously? How does this reward relate to the treasures mentioned in verses 19-21?

Matthew 10:34-42 (vs. 41, 42)
Who are the rewards given to in these verses? What are the rewards?

I Corinthians 3 (vs. 14)
What kind of spiritual construction work will receive a reward?

DAY 35

"I will . . ."

Reading: Hebrews 6:1-12 (vs. 10)

Dr. Henry Clay Morrison picked up his belongings at the train depot and made his way back home alone. "Nobody really cares!" Morrison thought. Born in Kentucky (1857), at the age of 11, he became a Christian and felt the call to ministry. Morrison eventually entered ministry as a Methodist minister and evangelist. His career was extensive; gospel tent-meeting preacher, founding editor of the paper entitled, "The Old Methodist" (later becoming "The Herald"), President of Asbury College and Seminary, and a missionary speaker traveling the world. The famous orator, William Jennings Bryan, once said of Morrison; "He's the greatest pulpit orator on the American continent." But, despite these accomplishments, Henry Clay Morrison came home from a world-wide mission trip without any fan fare or recognition.

As Morrison's ship sailed into a New York harbor, it was not greeted by bands playing or any dignitaries and supporters. After an African Safari trip, Teddy Roosevelt came back to this kind of welcome. And, when Roosevelt boarded a train or departed from a train, there were people waiting for him with the same kind of reception! When Morrison arrived at the harbor, and when he boarded his train for home, the governor, mayor, throngs of supporters didn't greet him!

After Morrison departed the train, feeling sorry for himself, he contrasted the kind of welcome Teddy Roosevelt had when he returned to his *own* welcome home. He thought to himself, "Here

I've been away from my family, have preached at many different ports, and have lead people to Christ on this trip—and, yet, there I was without a soul to meet me! Nobody cared. But then I stopped. A new glorious truth gripped me. And I found myself saying aloud, slowly, and exultantly, 'Henry, you're not really home yet'!"

Sometimes we might grow discouraged thinking that our contributions in the world are a waist of time because they go unnoticed and unappreciated. Or, we wonder why we put ourselves out for others, sacrificing time, resources, and even our own health when no one is standing by the train station waving flags and playing instruments in our honor.

Take these words from the New Testament to heart: "Though outwardly we are wasting away, yet inwardly we are being renewed day by day. For out light and momentary troubles are achieving for us an eternal glory that far outweighs them all. So fix your eyes not on what is seen, but on what is unseen. For the fanfare, red carpet, and ticker tape parades of this world are temporary, what is unseen is eternal." Friends, don't lose heart, you're not quite home yet! There are many of God's "I will . . ." promises contained in the Bible. Enjoy reading just a few of them this week and remember that God's "I will(s)" are for you today, through Jesus Christ (II Cor.1:20).

For further study and discussion

Genesis 12:1-7 (vs. 7)
How did Abram respond to God after he was given this future promise? How should we respond to God's future promises?

Jeremiah 15:1-11 (vs. 11)
What was the context of God's promise to Jeremiah? How does God's promise encourage Jeremiah? How does this same promise encourage us today?

Matthew 11:25-30 (vs. 28)
Does this promise include tired and weary servants of the Lord? What kind of "yokes" have become burdens to you in your life?

Matthew 16:13-20 (vs. 18, 19)
How would this promise encourage Peter in the future?

Hebrews 8 (vs. 8-12)
Have the promises in verses 8-12 been fulfilled today, or fulfilled in part?

Revelation 2:1-11 (vs. 10)
What is the reward for faithful service according to verse 10? Is this a present or future reward? Or both?

DAY 36

Fearfully and Wonderfully Made

Reading: Psalm 139:13-16

The Chicago Art Museum was given 2000 chalk drawings by a widow whose husband had collected older pieces of art. Many of these drawings were in bad shape and were stored in the basement of the museum until just recently. The museum had decided to catalog each piece of art they had in the basement. One of the pieces they came across was a picture of a hand painted by the great painter, Raphael. Assuming it was a reprint, a reprint of such a picture in good shape might be worth a few hundred dollars.

Come to find out, it wasn't a reprint! So, the museum staff thought that perhaps it was an original copy of the hand-painting done by one of Raphael's students. In this case, the painting would be worth thousands of dollars. The museum took the painting to an expert on Raphael paintings to have it appraised. But, the art scholar surprised the museum officials with the news that this painting was the original painting of Raphael, dating back into the early 1500s!

A painting the museum thought was worth a few hundred dollars, or a few thousand dollars, was now worth millions of dollars! Why the change in values? Value depends upon the one who created it. Sometimes we feel valueless or useless as people. We hate the way we look, or we think that we have nothing to offer, or we view ourselves with a measure of disgust when compared to others. Maybe we even wonder to ourselves, "Who would appraise me as being valuable, because I surely don't value myself very high!"

In Psalm 139, David, the King of Israel, writes not only about himself, but all of us when he says, "We are fearfully and wonderfully made." He believed that he was created by one who was more important and talented than the Great Raphael. God fashioned and knitted him together in his mother's womb. God gave him his abilities, his appearance, his personality, and an eternal soul. That makes David, and all of us human beings, priceless!

The next time you feel worthless, I suggest you consider getting another appraisal. Ask the Lord to show you His appraisal. You'll be surprised how much you're really worth—when He shows you the cross on which His only begotten Son died for your redemption!

For further study and discussion

Genesis 1:26-31 (vs. 26, 27)
What does it mean to be made in God's image according to this passage?

Genesis 9:1-7
Why is murder forbidden in this passage? Is murder an act of violence against God?

Psalm 8 (vs. 5)
What does this Psalm say about our position in the world? How are you exercising authority over creation?

I Corinthians 15:35-49 (vs. 49)
What kind of bodies will we receive when Christ returns? What kind of life will we enjoy as Christians when we are made new?

Galatians 3:26-29 (vs. 26)
What is our new status as Christians? How do we receive this new status and how does it improve our relationship with other Christians?

Ephesians 2:1-10 (vs. 10)
What does it mean to be God's workmanship? Does God make mistakes or junk? Are you enjoying the specific work God has planed for you to do?

DAY 37

The Zeal of the Lord

Reading: Isaiah 9:1-7 (vs. 7)

Evil, and those who do evil things, will have a day of reckoning. God is righteous and just, and in control of all things. The zeal of the Lord will establish and uphold what is righteous and just, both now and forever more. A perfect example of this zeal of the Lord took place back in 1989, in the former communist nation of Romania. The Romanian people were oppressed by a ruthless dictator, Nicolae Ceausescu. Liberty or freedom was unheard of in Romania. But on December 17, 1989 a Hungarian Reformed Pastor, Laszlo Tokes, stood up to the soldiers that had come to arrest him. Pastor Tokes was joined by hundreds of people who had come to his church, forming a protective shield around him and his wife. A candle light march began as people took to the streets in support of the Pastor. However, the soldiers broke into the church and beat Pastor Tokes before they hauled him away. But the soldiers could not stop the avalanche of support and the masses of people who filled the streets of Timisoara.

Ceausescu left this growing revolution in the hands of his army while he and his wife took off for Iran, not knowing there were many sympathizers of religious freedom in his army. When Ceausecu returned, the country was in a total revolt! Ceausescu quickly organized a rally on December 21st in Bucharest. Such rallies were the venue by which Ceausecu tried to force people to follow him through pro-Ceausecu banners and other political rhetoric. But this rally turned sour for the communist leader.

Soon people were shouting, "Down with Ceausecu!" As Ceausecu and his supporters tried to regain the momentum of the rally, people booed and threw shoes at him. As the crowd became more forceful, people stormed the Central Committee building. Ceausecu and his wife barely escaped by helicopter. But, back on the streets, a sermon was preached by a Baptist pastor in the streets of Timisoara. He heard the shouts of people saying, "God exists! There is a God. There is a God who is with us!" And on those streets there was prayer and Christmas hymns sung for the first time in 40 years.

On Christmas Day church bells rang with joy. Ceausecu and his wife, who had not totally escaped from the hands of the Romanian people, were tried and found guilty of crimes against the people of Romania. Since Ceausecu denied the existence of God and forbid the people to express their faith and worship in Christ, the people thought it fitting to schedule his execution on that day. Hundreds volunteered to serve on the firing squad. Video images of the dictator and his wife sprawled in pools of their own blood were televised across Romania and around the world.*

For further study and discussion

II Kings 19:20-31 (vs. 31)
What is promised here to Hezekiah in verse 31? What is the context of this promise?

Psalm 69:1-21 (vs. 9)
David speaks of his zeal for the Lord's house. Who quotes this verse in the New Testament, and why?

Isaiah 26:1-15 (vs. 11)
Who is God "zealous" for in this passage? How did God demonstrate his "zeal" for us? How does He continue to demonstrate His zeal for us even today?

Isaiah 37:21-32 (vs. 32)
How does God's zeal accomplish what is promised in verse 32 (see vs. 36-38)?

Ezekiel 5:8-17 (vs. 13)
How does God demonstrate His zeal according to this passage? How does this relate to the justice of the Lord?

Joel 2:12-24 (vs. 18)
Are zeal and jealousy considered synonyms in the Bible? What is the Lord zealous to do here in this passage?

DAY 38

Lift up Your Heads!

Reading: Psalm 3 (vs. 3)

Sometimes the people around us can make us feel two feet tall. Have you ever had that with your boss? It seems as if you can't do anything right in his eyes. Or, what about your spouse; has he/she ever made you feel like a "nobody" because you didn't do something right? Sometimes even children get beaten down with the drum beat of negative words and hurtful labels.

In Fredrick Huegel's book entitled, "Forever Triumphant", the story is told of how General Jonathan Wainwright was captured by the Japanese during World War II. Wainwright was severely beaten and soon became a broken and hopeless man. But then the war ended with the surrender of the Japanese, and the news reached the prisoner of war camp where General Wainwright was being held captive. An officer from the United States Army came to the camp to personally tell General Wainwright about the surrender. And, because the Japanese surrendered, the General was now officially in command.

After the news was personally delivered to the General, it didn't quite sink in at first. Remember, his spirit and emotions were beaten down, and his dignity as a human being was taken from him. But as he walked back to his barracks, one of the Japanese guards began to mistreat him as he had done in the past. Wainwright, however, with a new perspective of victory declared authority. He told the Japanese guard who was really now in charge. And it wasn't the Japanese! From that moment on, he was in command.

As a Christian, the Lord tells us that we are a royal priesthood, a holy nation, and a chosen people. We are Sons and Daughters of the king. In fact, Psalm 3 tells us that God is not only our shield, but he bestows glory on us and he lifts our heads up high.

Is someone trying to break your spirit, or doing everything in their power to beat you down? Are you feeling as if you've lost your dignity and are even being deprived of hope? Remember that the Lord is the one who can lift up your head and remind you of who you really are! I invite you to turn to the Bible and see yourself from the Lord's perspective. Why listen to the world's constant negative assessment of who you are, when in His eyes you are royalty!

For further study and discussion

Leviticus 26:1-13 (vs. 13)
What enabled the children of Israel to hold their heads up high?
What yoke needs to be broken in your life so that you can hold
your head up high?

Psalm 110 (vs. 7)
Who is David describing here in this passage? How or when will
this person "lift up his head"?

Psalm 113 (vs. 7)
Do you feel like your life is in the ash heap today? How does God
lift us up out of the dust and ash heaps?

Psalm 145 (vs. 14)
What prerequisite is necessary before God lifts a person up from
their troubles?

Psalm 146 (vs. 8)
Who are the "bowed down" ones that are described in this Psalm?

Luke 21:5-28 (vs. 28)
Why will heads be lifted up when the Son of Man comes? Take some
time to imagine that day and what it might be like for Christians.

DAY 39

I am the Lord's

Reading: I John 3: 1-10 (vs. 1)

Do you ever feel unimportant? For example, you don't ever get asked to take care of the real big accounts at work. Perhaps you wonder if your spouse really appreciates your sacrifices. Or, it bothered you this year that not one of your family members sent you a birthday card. And, perhaps, compared to what your brother or sister in-law earns for a living, you feel like a failure?

I'm reminded of a story about a young boy who went down to the Mississippi River one day to watch one of those ornate and majestic paddle boats float down the river. The boy came across an old man who was fishing by the river. The precocious little boy, with a Huck-Fin kind-of-voice asked the man, "What you doing mister?" "Fishing and I ain't caught a thing all day," the old man growled. The boy was about to give the older man a few tips on fishing when they heard the whistle of the mighty River Queen paddle boat coming down the Mississippi River. It was a beautiful boat, and it often carried many important people up and down the Mississippi.

Suddenly, the little boy shouted out as loud as he could, "Give me a ride! Give me a ride!" The old man turned to the little boy with bib overhauls and a dirty face, saying, "That boat is not going to stop for you! The River Queen is too important of a boat to stop and give rides to little boys." But the boy was persistent, crying out at the top of his lungs, "Let me ride! Let me ride!"

But then, the ship changed course and headed right toward the bank where the little boy was yelling. The old man's eyes bulged as that grand old boat stopped right in front of them, lowering the gang plank for the little boy to come aboard. As the old man continued to stare in disbelief, the little boy shouted back to the old man, "I knew the River Queen would stop for me! The captain is my daddy!"

Do you feel unimportant today? Perhaps it's time to look at yourself from God's perspective. When He looks at you, who or what does He see? Are you one of his sons or daughters? If so, He'll do more than just turn a river boat around for you. As His children, we are "lavished" with His love (Romans 8:32), and will continue to be doted upon for all eternity.

For further study and discussion

Psalm 17 (vs. 8)
What two beautiful images describe the Father's love for us, His children? What does it mean to be in the "shadow of His wings"?

Zechariah 2 (vs. 8)
Who is the "apple" of God's eyes here in this passage? What does it mean to be the "apple" of someone's eyes?

John 1:1-12 (vs. 12)
Can you name, or list, the spiritual blessings the Lord has given to you over this past year?

Romans 8:12-21 (vs. 21)
How will creation's freedom be a blessing to God's children when all things have been liberated in the future?

I Peter 2:4-12 (vs. 9, 10)
How does Peter describe Gods children here in this passage? How should we respond to the great love the Lord has "lavished" upon us, His children?

I John 5:13-21 (vs. 19)
How should children of the Lord live in a world under the control of the evil one?

DAY 40

No Disappointments!

Reading: I Thessalonians 2:17-20 (vs. 19)

If you ever watch the movie, "Mr. Holland's Opus", you'll get a little taste of what heaven might be like. Glenn Holland was a frustrated composer who never found the time to fulfill his lifetime goal: to write a concerto or opus. As a classical musician, he never received his claim to fame. He ended up taking a teaching position in Portland Oregon as a high school band director. Toward the end of the movie, Mr. Holland is forced to leave because of budget cuts to the music and art programs in the school. He taught kids music for 35 years, and now he was being let go. After all of the years of inspiring students to use their talents, what did he have to show for it?

As he cleans out his desk on the last day of school before summer break, he walks past the auditorium, hearing voices of people. And as he opens the doors to find out what was going on, he sees a capacity audience of former students and friends with a banner which read, "Goodbye Mr. Holland." The students and friends stood to their feet with a rousing ovation. The band, both former and present students, played songs he had taught for years. Even the Governor of the state of Oregon was in attendance! The Governor was a former student, encouraged by Mr. Holland in her first year of high school.

As the crowd calmed down, the governor took to the podium and reminded him that he had touched the lives of many students over the years. And while he never wrote a famous concerto or his opus, he had accomplished something far greater. The crowded auditorium proved her point.

What a powerful and even victorious surprise this was for Glenn Holland. But that's nothing compared to the surprise awaiting Christians in heaven. Jesus taught us to store up treasures in heaven. These treasures are people that are and will be in heaven because of our faithful and obedient witness to them. It's going to be an amazing day when God opens up the doors of heaven and introduces these people to us! Some we won't know, or even remember. But they'll be in heaven because God used your life, words, and even your resources to make an eternal difference in someone's life.

Don't ever underestimate the impact you have on others when you live your life for the Lord. Paul's joy, even with a sudden departure from Thessalonica, was that he would see these people again in glory. He would see his "spiritual offspring" in heaven. What a day of rejoicing it will be, both for Paul and for all who place their hope in the Lord.

For further study and discussion

Psalm 22 (vs. 5)
Were the Israelites ever disappointed with God's blessings? What usually caused their disappointment? Have you ever been disappointed with God's blessings in your life?

Isaiah 42:1-9 (vs. 4)
God's people will not be disappointed with His future servant because (see vs. 3) . . .

Isaiah 49:22-26 (vs. 23)
What is the prerequisite for being confident God will never disappoint us?

Matthew 25:14-30 (vs. 21, 23)
How does this passage encourage you to keep serving the Lord?

Hebrews 11:11-16 (vs. 16)
Why is God not ashamed to be called "their God"? What was their hope as they faithfully served the Lord?

Revelation 21:1-8 (vs. 4)
What is the "old order" of things (see vs.8)? What part of eternity do you look forward to the most?

*NOTES

1. Mitch Albom, **Tuesday's with Morrie** (Broadway, 2002)
2. Phyllis Thompson, **A Transparent Woman: The compelling story of Gladys Aylward** (Grand Rapids: Zondervan, 1971)
3. Jim Cymbal, **Fresh Wind, Fresh Fire** (Grand Rapids: Zondervan Pub., 1997)
4. Phyllis Ten Elshof, **What Cancer Cannot Do: Stories of Hope and Encouragement** (Grand Rapids: Zondervan Pub., 2006)
5. Lisa Beamer and Ken Abraham, **Let's Roll!** (Tyndale House Pub., 2002)
6. C.S.Lewis, **The Voyage of the Dawn Treader** (London: Geoffrey Bles, 1952)
7. Corrie Ten Boom with John and Elizabeth Sherril, **The Hiding Place** (Grand Rapids, Chosen Books, 1971)
8. J.R.R. Tolkien, **The Silmarillion** (George Allen and Unwin, 1977)
9. C.S. Lewis, **Prince Caspian** (New York: Macmillan Pub., 1951)
10. Chuck Colson, **The Body** (Dallas: Word Publishing, 1992)